POPULAR PARROTS

African Grey Parrot *(Psittacus erithacus)*

Peach-faced Lovebirds (*Agapornis roseicollis*), are among the most familiar of all Lovebirds and popular both as pets and as breeding birds for serious aviculturists. These African birds often demonstrate the charm associated with all the members of the parrot tribe.
Vriends

Popular Parrots

by

Dr. Matthew M. Vriends

First Edition — Second Printing

1984

HOWELL BOOK HOUSE INC.
230 Park Avenue
New York, N.Y. 10169

Library of Congress Cataloging in Publication Data

Vriends, Matthew M., 1937—
  Popular parrots.

  Bibliography: p. 239
  1. Parrots   2. Parrots—Identification.   I. Title.
SF473.P3V74   1983   636.6′865   83-10832
ISBN 0-87605-819-5

Contents

Black-cheeked Lovebirds (Agapornis p. nigrigenis)

Dr. Matthew M. Vriends

About The Author

For MATTHEW M. VRIENDS, an abiding interest in the animal kingdom is a family affair that spans the generations.

A native of Eindhoven in the southern Netherlands, Dr. Vriends was strongly influenced by his father's example and involvement in the sciences. The elder Vriends was a celebrated writer and respected biology teacher. An uncle also loomed large in the Dutch scientific community, and the Natural History Museum at Asten, which annually welcomes over 200,000 visitors, is named in his honor.

Dr. Vriends vividly remembers the field trips he shared with both father and uncle and the "mini menagerie" maintained in the Vriends family home. The facilities for keeping and observing flora and fauna included a pair of large aviaries housing over 50 tropical bird species. A source of particular pride is the fact that many *first breeding results* came about in the Vriends family aviary.

Dr. Vriends' first published material appeared in magazines while he was still in high school. He wrote and illustrated his first bird book at age 17—an amazing achievement that got young Vriends officially named the youngest biologist with a published work to his credit. This book was also an unqualified publishing success with more than six reprints and sales in excess of 40,000 copies!

During his University career, Matthew Vriends continued to publish literary essays, poetry, short stories, a number of fine bird books and even a novel that helped finance his education.

After graduation he worked as a high school teacher, but eventually left

11

education to devote more time to the serious study of ornithology. His work took him to some of the world's most exotic ports of call in Africa, South America, Indonesia and Australia. And it was in Australia—home of many of the world's most beautiful and unusual bird species—that Matthew Vriends became fascinated with native parrots, parakeets and grassfinches. He remained in Australia from 1964 through 1967 absorbed in study and continuous publication of ornithological subjects.

A number of the books published during these years came to the attention of Dr. Franz Sauer, world-famous ornithologist, who succeeded in persuading Dr. Vriends to come to the University of Florida at Gainesville. Here Vriends worked with world-renown biologists and to broaden his horizons, worked at the veterinary science and medical laboratories. One credit of which the author is particularly proud is having been allowed to work on the influenza virus research being conducted at that time.

Matthew Vriends earned his American doctorate in 1974 with a thesis on the Australian Masked Grassfinch (*Poephila personata*), and returned to Holland following the completion of his studies. Some time later he crossed the ocean again to take a position as the senior ornithology editor with a large American publishing firm until family concerns necessitated yet another return to the Netherlands in 1980. Vriends remained based in Holland until mid-1983 where he worked as an educator with additional interests in publishing and writing. He and his family now make their home on Long Island.

He remains an avid world-traveler, and, with his wife Lucy and daughter Tanya, regularly visits various countries of the world to observe the local wildlife close-up. His extensive travel also includes an annual journey to the United States where he is as well-known and respected by the American avicultural community as by the Dutch.

As his father did, Matthew Vriends maintains a large, varied collection of animals in his home for both enjoyment and study. Fish, hamsters, gerbils, mice, rats, guinea pigs, turtles, dogs and, of course, birds—some 80 different species—constitute the current Vriends family menagerie. Happily, it appears that Tanya Vriends will be the third generation biologist/aviculturist in the family as she joins her parents with great enthusiasm in their interest.

Dr. Vriends generously shares his expertise in various ways. A popular international judge, he frequently officiates at bird shows in many countries. At home he is the host of a weekly radio program and conducts seminars on birds and other animals in conjunction with trade show appearances during his American visits. His greatest fame has come through his writing and the helpful information he has imparted to pet owners and fanciers far and wide.

Currently Dr. Vriends is the author of some 80 books, in three languages, on birds, mammals, bees, turtles and fish, and over 1000 articles that have appeared in American and European magazines.

This remarkably prolific individual also enjoys music, painting, sketching, photography, tennis and gardening during rare moments of leisure when his attention is not directed to the natural sciences.

Dr. Matthew M. Vriends' accomplishments are like those of few others. By his varied activities in his chosen field, he has enlarged the body of knowledge for scientists, naturalists, diverse fancier groups and pet lovers around the world. His international celebrity is earned through more than thirty years of education, achievement and enthusiastic devotion to science and aviculture.

Hyacinth Macaw *(Anodorhynchus hyacinthinus)*

13

The Galah *(Eolopus roseicapillus)* is one of Australia's most plentiful Cockatoos and is in fact widening its natural range at this time. *Vriends*

Preface

$\mathbf{K}$EEPING AND CARING FOR PARROTS is remarkably popular at present, in spite of governmental regulations protecting rare species. These highly intelligent birds fully deserve this popularity.

To meet the wishes of many fanciers an introduction has been compiled which deals with the most essential aspects of how to keep and care for these birds—and, if possible, how to breed them.

Apart from some outdated books there are only a few (costly) handbooks that may be consulted. Existing literature from abroad, especially German and Dutch literature, is not accessible to everyone, partly also because of the high purchase costs.

Through my long acquaintance with these birds I can highlight those very important aspects essential for keepers of psittacines to know. Every good fancier strives to house and feed the parrots in his care so they can be kept as companions—in radiant health and full of enjoyment of life for many years. The care and eventual breeding of parrots must be done conscientiously. Individuals, zoos, and bird collections owe it to themselves and posterity to maintain the existing population, and, hopefully, add to it by breeding from available material. The wildlife situation is—as we all know—in great danger; whole areas in Africa and South America have fallen prey to so-called cultural progress. It is not the many parrot lovers that threaten the wildlife population (as is often unjustly claimed) but it is rather the often incorrect reclamations of land, the often unnecessary constructions of roads and fly-overs (even in our country examples of this can be cited!) or the destruction and fires caused by perpetual warfare.

The true aviculturist can perhaps help bring affected bird populations (through no fault of his own) back to the mark. May this book be a contribution, however modest, towards this realization.

Naturally this book was not written only for aviculturists; by adhering to correct ornithological taxonomy, the book is also a reference for biologists, ornithologists and anyone who because of profession or choice is involved with these interesting, intelligent animals. To assure the most accurate information, I have referred to Joseph M. Forshaw's standard work *Parrots of the World* (Lansdowne Press, Melbourne, Australia, Second Edition, 1978). This authoritative work, which should be an integral part of any ornithologist's library, enjoys general celebrity as an excellent reference work.

Suggestions or remarks which may improve or add to this text are welcome and may be used in a second edition.

That this book may help to enrich the lives of both fancier and birds is the sincere wish of . . .

. . .MATTHEW M. VRIENDS

Illiger's Macaw *(Ara maracana)* is an attractive representative of the "dwarf" macaw group. This species has been familiar to aviculture since the early 19th century and there have been a number of successful captive breedings reported.   *Vriends*

16

Acknowledgements

I wish to thank all those who have assisted in the production of this book, particularly Mr. R. Ceuleers and Mrs. P. Leijsen, of Herentals, Antwerp, Belgium; Mrs. Ruth Hanessian of "Animal Exchange," Rockville, Maryland; Mr. E.P.J. Meijer, of Alpen, Holland, Mr. G. Ebben of the University of Nijmegen; and Mr. M. Ridder of "Bogena," Waalwijk, Holland, for their great help, and those who have allowed me to use their photographs, especially my dear friend Mr. A. Sloots, of Upwey, Victoria, Australia, and Mr. Ad. Kers, of Waalwijk, Holland. This book could not have been produced without the help of these and other fine people!

I would also like to acknowledge my indebtedness to my wife, Mrs. Lucy Vriends-Parent, for her invaluable assistance and patience during the preparation of the text; the many discussions we had about this book have formed the basis of much of my own attitude to the practical aspects of the subject.

All the opinions and conclusions expressed in the text are my own, however, and any errors must be my own responsibility.

M.M.V.

NOTE: This book expresses small linear and liquid measurements in their metric and English forms. For the guidance of readers not yet completely familiar with the metric equivalents of standard English and American measurements the following conversion information should prove helpful:

One meter (m) is equal to 1000 millimeters (mm). A centimeter (cm) contains 10 millimeters and is 1/100 of a meter. One inch is equal to about 2.5 cm or 25 mm. Four inches are about equal to 100 mm; 6 inches = 150 mm; 1 foot = 305 mm; 3 feet = 914 mm. The number of millimeters divided by 10 gives the number of centimeters.

To convert degrees Centigrade (or if you prefer Celsius) to degrees Fahrenheit, multiply degrees Centigrade by 1.8, and then add 32. ($^\circ$C x 1.8) + 32 = $^\circ$ F. Some good base temperatures to remember are: 0° C = 32° F; 10° C = 50° F; 20° C = 68° F; 30° C = 86° F; 100° C = 212° F.

Parrot-family birds are universally famous for their tremendous agility. As demonstrated by this Blue and Gold Macaw, the acrobatic ability of these birds sometimes even rivals that of monkeys. *Vriends*

POPULAR PARROTS

The Australian King Parrot is one of the most colorful
and spectacular of all Australian psittacines. *Leysen*

1

An Introduction to Birds

ORNITHOLOGY is the study of birds in the broadest sense of the word. An aviculturist could well call himself an ornithologist if he studies birds with regard to their general behavior, breeding and nesting habits, and rearing young. Although he is only studying a small part of this branch of zoology, he is still concerned with the observation, record keeping, and study of the birds in his care. The professional ornithologist goes a step further and may be involved with studying the structure of various species; he digs deeply into the physiology, life style and behavior, classification, and distribution of birds in an attempt to come up with new and/or further information. Presumably, even prehistoric man studied birds, judging from cave drawings dating back to that era. We also learn from the Bible that there have always been people involved with the study of birds. Among the works of Aristotle (384-322 B.C.) there was a classification of birds. Because there are so many genera with countless representatives (over 8,500 species) and because birds can be recognized quite readily, many scholars and fanciers alike have become expert ornithologists. Birds are widely studied because of a certain magnetism people feel toward them. Their lovely colors or their interesting behavior patterns during breeding or migration periods add to the attraction. Purely practical reasons also have a bearing on avian significance, such as their economic importance as a food source or because they help exterminate harmful insects. Therefore, it is appropriate to start this book with a small chapter on ornithology, affording some insight into what is common to all birds.

General Considerations

Birds belong to the great Vertebrate division (subphylum of phylum *Chordata*) of the animal kingdom. They are warm-blooded (or *homoiothermic*) and their upper limbs have been formed into wings. An important characteristic of all birds is the presence of feathers covering the skin. Almost all birds can fly and *all* species lay eggs as part of their reproductive cycle. The front of the skull has been elongated to form a beak or bill, of which the upper mandible cannot be moved; exceptions to this rule, among others, are the psittacines and birds of prey.

In reality, the feathers are the only visible trademark that sets birds apart from other vertebrate animals. Feathers are formed by the skin. The skin itself is very loosely fitted around the body and is very dry, since there are no sweat glands. When a bird is feeling rather warm it sits with its beak open. The feathers form a beautiful insulating layer covering the entire body except for the legs and feet (some exceptions here, too). Feathers help maintain a constant body temperature and act as a water repellent. The wings are very well-developed and serve as a flight instrument for most birds; some can even use them very successfully when fighting—and when we say "fighting" we mean two birds striking each other with their wings! The wings generally cover a surprisingly large area and are extremely light in weight.

Feathers

When we observe a flight feather, we see a kind of coil of loose down attached to it where it becomes the quill; the quill itself having a "flag" both to the right and left. The flag consists of barbules held together by small hooklets, which indeed are hooks that fit exactly into an indentation of the barbule in front. The advantage of this piece of engineering is that whenever the feather becomes a little ruffled or damaged through flying or other causes, the bird can straighten it simply by running his beak through the feather.

All flight feathers are attached to muscles which can alter the angle of the feathers. This can be clearly seen when a bird which is ill sits shivering with puffed-up feathers in the corner of cage or aviary. Feathers also have a nerve connection which can cause a prickling effect when the feathers are touched, comparable to the whiskers of a cat.

The down feathers are very soft and, since they are located close to the body, serve to hold the warm air near the skin. In contrast, the flight feathers and coverts are broad and flat, and give a bird its shape, which is usually something like a torpedo. These larger feathers also serve to give some protection against the penetration of the flowing air. As previously mentioned, the feathers give the bird a streamlined shape during flight, and the entire skeletal structure accentuates this as well.

Birds' legs and toes are covered with scales, a holdover from their forebears, the reptiles. These scales fit over each other.

Another remarkable feature is their so-called "third eyelid," a trans-

The Red-fronted Macaw (Ara rubrogenys) shows an interesting variation from most other Macaw species in the almost total absence of the typical, bare cheek patch. In *A. rubrogenys* this patch is limited to a small area just below the eye. *Leysen/Vriends*

23

parent disc known scientifically as the *nictitating membrane,* which moves straight across the eye. This eyelid can be clearly observed with dozing or just-awakened birds.

Flying

Why is a bird so well-suited for flying? The first reason, of course, is the upper limbs modified as wings and covering a large area thanks to the feathers. The second reason, I would say, is the large breast muscles which pull down the wings. In many bird species these muscles often represent more than one-fifth of the bird's total weight.

Next I would draw your attention to the breastbone to which these muscles are attached. The extremely well-developed coracoid bones (from New Latin *coracoides* "bone shaped like a crow's beak") are also well-worth mentioning, because these transfer the propelling power of the wings to the body. Noteworthy, too, is the sturdy, stiff skeleton which serves as a framework to which the flight muscles are attached. As an example, the posterior vertebrae have been fused together and cannot be moved separately, which is not the case among other vertebrates, including mammals. The bones are hollow, greatly reducing body weight and contributing to flight efficiency. Finally the "wind bags," which we will discuss in more detail a little later, are also important.

Propulsion

Although not all bird species use the same manner of propulsion in flight, it is safe to say that birds in general can execute an active flight. We understand this to be a "thrust and row" flight, and a passive "sailing and gliding" flight. Many bird species, incidentally, use these types of propulsion in various ways.

What is meant by active flight? The word "active" implies that the movement is not entirely involuntary, but that the bird itself is doing something. With a thrusting flight the bird pulls his breast muscles together, causing the wings to go down. The resistance of the air against the stretched out wing causes the upward propulsion. This propulsion is transferred through the coracoid bones to the sternum and continues through the center of gravity of the bird, causing the entire bird to become airborne. According to McKean there is, in addition to the upward thrust, also a forward propulsion generated through the flipping down of the primaries at the time that the wings are brought down, which then works as a propeller, particularly at the upper part of the wing. When the wings are thrust down, the forward edge of the wing lies lower than the back edge, causing the air to be pushed backward and the bird therefore is pushed forward. Speaking in general terms, we can say that the secondaries are involved in the upward motion, while the primaries are largely responsible for the forward motion. The alula (group of small feathers at the bend of the wing) can be important when a bird

A group of Macaws consisting of two Green-wings (left) and three Blue and Golds. In general, the Macaw species are very compatible and there has even been some hybridization carried out with interesting and beautiful results.   *Vriends*

takes off, because it can generate some forward propulsion, and during flight it can maintain an even airstream above the wing area. The upward thrust of the wings is executed faster than the downward thrust. A smaller chest muscle contracts to bring the wings upward, since the tendon runs through an opening in the shoulder to the upper part of the upper arm bone. Quite often the arm is only turned a little, so that the front is higher than the back edge and the air stream lifts the bird upwards. The wing is bent at the wrist during the upward thrust, thereby reducing the amount of resistance. In addition, the manner in which the primaries and secondaries are designed, one overlapping the other like tiles on a roof, causes a maximum of resistance during the downward thrust and a minimum during the upward thrust.

With the gliding flight, the wings are stretched out and used as a sail, causing the bird to glide downward along the "air cushion," losing altitude and gaining a forward momentum. Sometimes rising warmer air streams (thermics) or gusts of wind can be used to gain altitude (sailing flight) without the use of wing motions, such as is done by seagulls, buzzards and large parrots. In general, swift-flying birds have a small wing surface area and a large wing span with particularly well-developed primaries, while slower birds have shorter, broader wings with well-developed secondaries.

From these somewhat technical notations, for which the author is grateful to Mr. McKean, we can conclude that the speed of flight can vary a great deal from species to species. A very fast flier is the swift (*Apus apus*), which can attain a speed of some 160 kilometers (approximately 99 miles) per hour! A carrier pigeon, on the other hand, takes it a little easier, doing about 60 (approximately 37 miles) k.p.h.

Of course the tail feathers help stabilize the flying bird, while they also perform an important function during braking and landing.

With regard to walking, because of the posture of a bird the center of gravity falls under the joint of the thigh bone and pelvis, which is particularly obvious when observing the walk (more like a waddle) of ducks and other waterfowl.

Respiration

Every bird, be it an ostrich or a parrot, has relatively small lungs which differ in a number of factors from those of man and other mammals. They are not elastic, for starters, and do not have any small air pockets; in place of these we find countless branches which eventually unite in air passages. These are virtually encircled with hair follicles. The lungs are attached at the back side of the chest cavity.

Before air enters the lungs it is first inhaled, of course, and comes through the windpipe or trachea. This is a long tube held open by rings of cartilage. It runs from the beak to the body cavity where, just as in man, it splits into two short branches (bronchi), each of which empties into the lungs. The bronchus in turn splits into many progressively smaller tubes which pierce through the lung tissue and empty into the air sacs as tubes. These air sacs have extremely

26

thin walls and fit exactly into the cavity; they precisely fill the cavity between the organs and the muscles located there. Most species possess ten air sacs— five pairs. The air sacs located toward the back are generally the largest.

We already know that the breast bone (or sternum) is pulled upward when a bird is in flight; consequently the internal space is considerably reduced with the pulling together of the chest muscles. Through this decrease in size it follows that the air sacs are pushed in a little, so that air is pushed from the windpipes of the lungs to the bronchi, from there to the trachea, and out through the nostrils. The chest muscles restore the body cavity to normal size during relaxation, so that air can again be sucked into the air sacs through the bronchi.

There are only a relatively small number of blood vessels present in the air sacs so, understandably, only little absorption of oxygen is realized; on the other hand, when the oxygen arrives in the lungs through the small tubes, the many hair follicles absorb oxygen in their walls and expel carbonic acid. McKean said this was a very efficient manner of obtaining oxygen and expelling carbonic acid because there is no "dead space"; fresh air is rapidly transported throughout the lungs and exchange takes place twice, both on the way in and the way out. Because the most powerful flight movements also compress the air sacs most, the increased intake of oxygen fulfills the increased need of the active muscles and speeds up the removal of carbonic acid. When a bird is not in flight, the ribs are moved by muscles which squeeze the body cavity and then release again, thereby forcing air in and out of the windbags. Under normal circumstances the muscles are actively involved with exhalation, while with mammals it is the inhalation that is caused by the pulling together of the muscles.

Many secondary details have not been mentioned. I don't wish to go too deeply into these, such as the fact that the oxygen that makes its way into the air sacs in the back part of the body through a rather complicated passage (namely through the lungs to the air sacs located in the front of the bird's body) is expelled through the nostrils, with a great many "valves" preventing the back-flow of air. Many diving water birds have the ability to send oxygen back and forth several times from one pair of windbags to the next until most of the oxygen has been absorbed by the lungs.

Peach-faced Lovebirds *(Agapornis roseicollis)*, go to nest readily and so make a good species to work with for the beginning bird breeder.   *Ebben*

2

Parrots in Home and Garden

WHEN YOU WISH to acquire a parrot, first ask yourself whether you will have sufficient time, space and (perhaps most important) enough interest; is it an impulse, a fad? Ask yourself what exactly is your intention: a bird that is tame and is able to chat away, or do you desire an animal that is striking in its attachment to you, or do you perhaps plan to breed birds?

The African Grey Parrot and the beautiful Amazon Parrots undoubtedly have great imitating talent; the Cockatoos have an affinity for learning to perform tricks, possess gentle characters and are also friendly to children.

The best breeding results are obtained with certain species of Lovebirds and other dwarf parrots. If you want a bird in the home you would do well to inquire prior to purchase, whether the bird has a habit of screeching. Believe me, there are some really noisy animals among the above-mentioned birds. But even a bawler will grow calm, when he is kept on his own *and* if the fancier is willing to spend much time with him every day.

The Cage

Only spacious cages in which the bird can move about freely, should be purchased; avoid round cages as these can make the birds nervous, but rectangular or square models will do well. The bars should run horizontally, so that the bird can climb. A climbing-pole in the form of a large branch should be erected in the cage as a few artificial perches are not sufficient. Only

The Citron-crested Cockatoo is an interesting subspecies of the Lesser Sulphur-Crested Cockatoo. It makes a very satisfactory house pet and an adaptable aviary resident. *Kers*

The Lesser Sulphur-crested Cockatoo also makes a fine aviary bird, while its size is convenient for those who live in apartments and would like to keep a Cockatoo. *Kers*

tame birds that spend much time outside their cages in play pens and similar enclosures, can, if desired, be placed in a round cage. As for the size you can apply a rule of thumb: the birds must be able to flap their wings without their running the risk of injuring or breaking their feathers. Macaws and other long-tailed parrots should therefore have elongated cages, otherwise their tails will be broken in no time and the birds will appear unattractive.

Water containers and seed dishes should be firmly attached to the bars, to the climbing-pole or elsewhere and in such a way that the bird cannot loosen them which it will undoubtedly try to do.

Many cages have double bottoms, the top of which is constructed of wire grating. Personally I am not in favor of these, as it is very difficult for the birds to walk on them, although there is something to be said for them from a hygienic point of view, especially in hospital cages.

If you have a cage with wire grating, it is advisable to cover half of it with grass-sod. This can be moistened daily; the birds will love to roll around in it and in so doing, bathe. But I prefer a solid bottom covered with grass-sod, partially with grit, and sand especially composed as ground-cover for cages, so that the bird may take in necessary minerals.

When a fancier desires to breed in the home he is able to choose from a wide assortment of breeding cages. Pay attention to the sturdiness of the material (parrots are strong chewers and can do much damage) and the size; a minimum of 30 inches (75 cm) length, a depth of 18 inches (45 cm) and a height of 20 inches (50 cm) is advisable. We should then encounter no further problems.

Stand and Climbing Trees

You can see parrots, especially tame individuals of the larger species (Macaws, Cockatoos and Amazons) on T-shaped or circular stands in zoos and bird gardens. A light leg chain prevents them from flying off into the sky. It is now illegal to keep parrots on stands with a foot-clamp. Often the leg to which the ring with the small chain was attached, was seriously injured or the ring cut deeply into the flesh when the leg grew. However most birds kept on stands were placed into cages for the night.

More recently climbing trees populated by large parrots are often seen. Here the birds sit together on the tree without being chained and if they wish can fly about a little. These birds are also placed in spacious cages in the evening.

It is obvious that a climbing tree can only be used for tame, trustworthy birds. Use a climbing tree with firm, thick branches and do not remove the bark. The birds will take care of this; it will present diversion and relaxation for them.

One more matter to consider: it is probably best to clip one wing of birds kept on a climbing tree so that you do not run the risk of their flying off permanently, for they are too expensive to permit that.

Cage Location

Cages and aviaries must have light and sun, but the birds must be able to escape from direct sunlight if they choose to do so. Rooms and gardens facing north are therefore totally unsuitable, as are those places labeled as a spot "to place Polly." I want to point out emphatically that sun and light are two essential factors for all birds, including parrots. If you were to meet these requirements with the help of expensive fluorescent lighting or with the so-called "sunlight" lamps, the negative influence on the birds would show sooner or later. I do not say that your birds will not be able to survive for a few years, for they certainly will; that is not the point here. To rear and care for birds also entails caring for life, and beauty. Birds that do not receive any sun will soon lose all gloss and color and will gradually pine away, becoming a pitiful heap of feathers. Too often I have seen expensive birds die very slowly, even though—and this must be said—the fancier had taken good care of everything apart from the aforementioned. It is exactly as with indoor plants: our care may be good and our knowledge extensive and excellent, but when we deprive plants of light and deprive many sorts regularly of sun, they will soon lose all beauty and will die a sad bunch of thin stems, to disappear in the trash. One requirement is therefore, that the front of a cage—assuming that you have a box cage or aviary—faces south, if it is even remotely possible. When this is not practical for whatever reason, then it should face southward as much as possible, and southeast rather than southwest. You would do well to construct part of the front, at least of the aviary, of double glass (not plate glass), and this is certainly necessary if the front is *not* facing south. Apart from this requirement of placement pay particular attention, when building an aviary in the garden, to build in a visible location, preferably with some flower beds, shrubs and such as environment and background. Actually the same applies for a cage; it should face south and if this cannot quite be arranged, it should face southeast rather than southwest. The show cage and the indoor aviary as well should face south as much as possible. The main thing is that the birds are able to enjoy the sun for a few hours every day.

In the home the aforementioned places also form excellent spots for indoor plants. With a little artistic insight we can arrange the birds' home and the plants in such a way that a natural composition is created. For nothing is so annoying as a cage or an aviary which strikes you as irritating. When I see how most parrot cages are placed, it makes my hair stand on end. Why does the cage always have to be placed exactly in the middle, in front of the window, just like a lighthouse on a small, bare island?

Cages should be situated in such a way that their inhabitants can look down upon us (literally speaking). As you know, birds are accustomed to fly away or to climb up in case of danger; a tendency they will always display when they are threatened by curious (and for them mostly totally strange) spectators, who view the cage from above.

It is much more sensible to place a cage in such a way that it is always slightly higher than an adult. If you follow my advice you will soon be able to note that the birds do not fly up nervously or beat their wings when we pay attention to them.

In connection with possible training it is, of course, desirable, that the birds are housed in as quiet a location as possible. Cages, when placed low, will usually house shy, restless inhabitants which try to hide themselves, so that the fancier will not enjoy his birds' company to the full. In the case of cages which house more than one bird, the inhabitants can sometimes influence each other to such an extent that they kick up a racket, and all the effort spent on training and instruction could be undone, because of this.

Finally, when the sun is too strong and burning, you can place the cage somewhere else, of course (but free from draft and wind), or cover it by means of a newspaper or a screen, especially made for this purpose.

Choosing the Right Cage

As observed earlier there is a wide choice in cages. Not all of these models are suitable, however. Any cage should be a proper home for your parrot. Elegance and shape are only of secondary importance.

Apart from the expense of obtaining a cage and other required paraphernalia take care not to spend all your money on such a "home." Your first thought should be to find a pair of parrot-like birds, as healthy as possible, and that make a lively impression. Only top quality birds are suitable. This certainly applies when you wish to buy only one bird, because when you cannot spend much time with him, the parrot must feel comfortable in his cage and be able to amuse himself for many hours (how he can amuse himself we will discuss later on).

If you wish to start with one bird—because you would like to teach it to speak—buy a young bird; one that has become physically independent, is in good health and whose feathers are in good condition. Examine a cage for practical criteria: the cage must be easy to clean; seed trays, water containers, perches and other furnishings should be within easy reach of both bird and owner. Painted or enamelled cages are, of course, not suitable for your purpose, as hookbills love to gnaw bars and similar objects, with disastrous results. The so-called antique cages, which may sometimes be found in second-hand stores, can sometimes look very rustic and attractive in the living room or study but are usually suitable only for the smaller bird species. Paint such cages, which are usually of wood, with a paint that is harmless for birds (do not use oil-based paint or paint that contains lead). Paints used for childrens' furniture suit this purpose very well. Birds can be placed in a renovated cage only after all paint is thoroughly dry; pay special attention to the corners, where paint collects. A serious disadvantage of these old cage models is that the many corners are easy hiding places for vermin, and are not so easy to clean. Twice yearly immerse the cage in water to which a disinfectant has been added, to destroy disease germs.

The Yellow-collared Macaw *(Ara auricollis)* belongs to the family of dwarf macaws and is approximately half as long as the larger Macaws. This species is named for the golden-yellow marking on its neck. *Ebben*

A recently-acquired cage should also first be washed in hot water, to which a disinfectant has been added. This is strongly recommended, as new cages are usually immersed in a certain type of acid to heighten their gloss.

In conclusion, when selecting a cage make sure that bars are not too far apart and that all, or most of them, are placed horizontally.

Pay particular attention to the distance between the bars. Many a bird died a cruel death, from getting stuck between the bars in an attempt to free itself from the cage, and suffocated.

I speak of horizontally placed bars, as parrots enjoy climbing, and this would be difficult to do in cages built with vertically placed bars.

Lovebirds and other dwarf parrots are generally lively creatures. That is why people sometimes use spacious parakeet cages for them which offer the opportunity to place toys in them (swings, carousels, ladders, horizontally and vertically hanging chains with small bells). The most modern cages of this type may even have a firm plastic tub-bottom, which greatly facilitates cleaning; the cage can be removed from the tub, without having to catch the birds first.

Hang a small mirror in the cage if you keep only one bird in it; dwarf parrots and Lovebirds are quite vain creatures. Aim at keeping two birds; preferably a couple, if it is at all possible, as they provide company for each other.

The mirror will prevent boredom for a single bird to a certain extent, especially during the long hours the animal has to wait before you return home and can give it attention.

Naturally you should position the perches in the cage so that the birds, sitting on them, cannot foul the food and water, nor each other. Do not place two perches immediately below each other for obvious reasons.

The so-called "tower-shaped" or "turret-shaped" cages, currently very popular, are round, small, high cages standing on three slender legs; the entire structure is about as high as an average 12-year-old child. For its height alone such a cage should be considered unsuitable and its shape also seems impractical for the comfort of your birds. There are a few more objections, but the above two are sufficient reasons to condemn this model. A couple of dwarf parrots or Lovebirds can amuse themselves very nicely in such a cage— especially if they are tame—partly because the bars run horizontally. But for other psittacines these cages are totally unsuitable, as flying is nearly impossible. Birds like to flap their wings and the tower-shaped cage will usually not allow for this.

The Box Cage

A bird feels most at ease in a cage that is partially closed: the so-called box cage. Such a cage has bars on the front only, but is otherwise closed. Currently ready-made models are available and some even come with built-in lighting. They are designed according to the same principles, and marketed under the more attractive name of "show cages." Of course, such a cage should be placed in a bright location (apart from the artificial lighting), but not in direct sunlight, as a cage of this type would soon become too hot. Box cages are eminently suitable for breeding, as they offer the nesting couple the most security. Thus many Lovebird species are very likely to breed in them.

You can often see these cages in halls and on porches. There is, of course, nothing against this, providing the cage is draft-free. Birds that are placed in drafty rooms may catch cold and can become seriously ill and die.

Box cages and their contemporary equivalents can serve well as winter residences for the smaller parrots housed in a spacious aviary throughout the spring and summer (and often part of the fall as well since that is when they start breeding).

Perches

Perches in cages must be placed in front of the seed trays and water containers. At best one perch should be placed high in the cage as parrots (like all other birds) love roosting as high as possible.

It is important not to fill the cage with too many perches. There should be plenty of space for the birds to move about. Moreover, you should not place the perches directly above one another, as mentioned earlier; birds roosting on the top perches may soil those sitting below.

Perches should not all be equally thick, for a variation in thickness will offer relaxation to the muscles of the leg and foot. Elder, willow, eucalyptus and small branches of fruit trees should not be lacking in *any* cage, and then particularly those branches that have bark on them. Always be sure not to use tree branches that have been sprayed with insecticides.

Sand on the Cage Bottom

Every well-constructed cage possesses a pull-out bottom tray to facilitate cleaning. Certain tub cages can be completely removed from their bottom. It is advisable to cover the drawer with a strong piece of brown paper or wrapping paper on top of which a ¼″ thick layer of shell sand is strewn. Avoid newspaper as the birds will gnaw on it and ingest harmful substances from the ink. Shell sand is sold on the market under various brand names, or a layer of grit can also be used. At least once a week this sand bottom should be replaced with a clean one, as well as the above-mentioned paper. To avoid or reduce spilling sand, attach glass or a clear plastic strip of about 4″ (10 cm) high around the cage. Usually they are standard equipment on a box cage, but tower cages are often sold without them, and you must install the strip or guard yourself.

Covering a Cage

Many fanciers believe that cages should be covered with a piece of cloth during the evenings and at night. Not every parrot, however, appreciates a covered cage.

36

In my opinion, it is best to cover one side only, or part of the roof, so that artificial light does not shine directly on the bird. The bird can then choose whether it would like to sit in the light or not.

Toys

Lovebirds and other smaller parrots will often amuse themselves with all kinds of playthings, and in that respect their nature resembles that of the Budgerigar. Every bird store or pet shop offers ample choices in this field, so you can make the bird happy quickly and simply.

Be mindful that too many toys in the cage will not exactly present a tidy sight and it may result in the birds becoming more interested in these knick-knacks than in you! This is a distraction to taming your parrots.

Personally I most prefer a small mirror with a bell attached to it, for Budgerigars and for dwarf parrots. Small ladders offer the birds necessary exercise, but should not decrease their flying space. Tame birds may be provided with playgrounds outside their cages, usually a square tray made of sheet metal or plastic, on which various toys can be placed; all parrot species will use this.

When the bird can be allowed outside the cage, a platform on the threshold seems useful, if not necessary. It makes it considerably easier for birds to enter the cage. This "runway" is best constructed of plywood and is easily constructed by anyone. We do run the risk of regularly having to make a new runway though, which shouldn't be too much effort, even for a clumsy person.

Safety Precautions

When you allow a parrot to fly anywhere about the home for a few hours, you must be sure all windows and doors are firmly closed, that the drapes have been drawn to prevent the bird from flying against the glass (all too often a cause of serious accidents), that the fireplace has been safely covered by a screen, and that all electric appliances and stoves have been switched off. Any fans in use on hot days should also be switched off or covered with screening, so the birds cannot get at them. Indoor plants and flowers may also cause problems; they form a potential danger for the birds. Parrots are very curious and are bound to inspect your plants sooner or later. As various plants are poisonous it is as well to keep vigilant. Plants such as cacti can cause serious injuries. Therefore, it is best to remove all plants from the room or to cover them temporarily with plastic.

Cleaning the Cage

The cage should always be kept spotlessly clean. This not only holds true for the cage itself, but also for the perches, the water, food and bathing dishes as well as any toys. It is best to establish a regular routine for cage cleaning by doing it, for example, once a week at a convenient time. At least once a month disinfect everything with the greatest possible care. To do so you will have to remove the birds from their cages. An extra cage, to be used as a temporary home at this time, will be very useful, if not a necessity. The cage is then cleaned thoroughly with hot water and afterwards rinsed with cold water, in which disinfectant is dissolved, so that disease germs are destroyed.

The same applies to all the utensils in the cage. Chipped glass containers and cracked plastic toys should be replaced as disease germs and bacteria may easily multiply in cracks and blemishes.

Bathing

Many species of parrots and parakeets delight in rolling about in moist grass, especially in the morning when the grass is still covered with dew. This is an unforgettable sight for the fancier.

In captivity this "bath in the morning" cannot always be provided, though we are able to achieve much in an aviary.

Bird stores sell small plastic or metal bathing tubs, that are actually intended for canaries, and tropical and sub-tropical cage birds. These can be hung over the cage threshold in the morning, or if desired, throughout the day. As these bathing tubs are far too small for the larger species, not all dwarf parrots will make use of them. Often they will take a "shower" at the water tray by quickly ducking their heads in the water and thus wash themselves. Wet grass sod on the bottom of the cage or a few wet lettuce leaves in the bathing dishes are always welcome, and often the birds' behavior will be highly amusing. Birds that are regularly allowed out of their cages will sooner or later discover your dripping kitchen faucet (and if it is not dripping you can let it drip); Lovebirds and Budgerigars are particularly keen on this.

When a bird has made a habit of taking a shower under the kitchen faucet it is important that the hot water tap remains firmly turned off.

If the birds dislike bathing, you must wash them yourself from time to time. When the birds are going to an exhibition you will also have to bathe your birds at least a week before the date of a show, preferably earlier. We only bathe birds when it is absolutely necessary.

As a bird's body is very fragile, be exceptionally careful about handling and holding it. Prepare, before taking the bird from its cage, two shallow bowls or plates with warm water (approx. 80° F) in which some soft soap has been dissolved. A good brand of dish detergent may also be used for this purpose. The bird should be held in the hand in such a way that you can support its head with your thumb and forefinger. Next the parrot should be immersed carefully in the bowl with the dissolved soap, in such a way that its head is not brought into contact with the water, in order to prevent soap from coming into its eyes, nose and bill. When you have immersed the animal several times in a calm and controlled manner, you can then take an old shaving brush with soft bristles which you wet first in the saucer with soap. With this you stroke the feathers in the direction of the tail. Do not forget the area around the anus (vent). You can clean the head and neck with a soft, non-synthetic sponge. Make certain not to rub soap into the bill, nose or eyes of the parrot. To give the wings a good wash, you can spread them across the edge of the plate; cleaning them is mere child's play. You can do the same with its tail, but take care to do this carefully to avoid accidental feather loss, which is ruinous for show birds (Amazon and dwarf parrots, particularly).

Lovebirds, with the exception of an extremely tame specimen, are never given such treatment, simply because they cannot bear it; it makes them nervous and they may even suffer shock.

The bowl with clean water is used to rinse the bird. Immerse the bird a few times in the water, and restore its shape with a clean brush, since obviously our treatment has ruffled the feathers a good deal.

Finally the bird must be dried, which is best performed by using a thick towel, that has been warmed a little.

After bathing and drying, the bird is placed in a clean, not-too-large cage, without sand, in a warm room. Never put the bird outside in the sun or too close to a stove. The bird should not be taken from this room until the following day to prevent him from catching cold. Make sure the room is not too hot either, for otherwise the feathers will curl, which is not your intention. A hair dryer may be helpful if you know how to use it, but you must remain in the immediate vicinity if you want to try the latter, to prevent accidents.

Mirrors in the Cage

Parrots, especially those housed alone in a cage, love to play with mirrors and to observe themselves from all sides. Use very strong, securely framed mirrors only, those that cannot be gnawed through, as obviously broken glass is a great hazard. Mirrors should be part of every cage. Lovebirds and other dwarf parrots simply adore mirrors. When the birds are allowed to fly about in the living room, even for an hour, be careful with any mirrors in the room, as these will invariably be inspected. When the birds are let free in the room for the first time, cover any mirror with a piece of cloth (and, for that matter, any window as well). After a few days, when the birds have become accustomed to the room you may remove this piece of cloth. So mirrors in cages are ideal for small hook-billed birds confined by themselves (which we try to avoid). There is, however, one disadvantage in giving mirrors to parrots. Sometimes the bird becomes so taken with its own reflection that it no longer has an eye for the other parrots, or its owner; it has fallen in love with itself.

I feel we should take this risk when the parrot is alone too much. If, after some time, it would appear that the bird is growing too interested in its own reflection, remove the mirror and replace it with some other toy. Obviously you should then pay extra attention to your little friend, to alleviate the loss of its "partner."

I have noticed that neither Lovebirds nor dwarf parrots soil their mirrors with regurgitated food, as Budgerigars do.

During breeding time parrot and parakeet pairs feed each other regurgitated food, which has nearly the same composition as that which is later fed to their young.

Ornamental clothespins have many uses in bird keeping. In recent years we have been able to find ornamental clothespins of about 6 inches (15 cm) in length) in various department stores and gift shops. These are designed to keep bills, letters and such together. Parrot and parakeet lovers may make good use of such ornamental clothespins for keeping cage doors open, for holding green foods, sprigs, toys, the important spray-millet, the small strip of carrot, and cuttlebone. They can also be used as perches, and have the advantage of being attachable as a roosting place almost anywhere.

In an aviary too they may be serviceable, particularly as an easy way of clipping green twigs to the wire mesh and between the breeding boxes or of attaching sisal rope, which birds like to climb. The latter is excellent therapy against boredom. There are undoubtedly various other possibilities which I will let you discover for yourself.

Special Summer Care

The main essential in bird keeping is scrupulous cleanliness. As temperatures become higher, it is very likely that any soft foods (nestling food, concentrated food, milk-soaked bread, green food or fruit) will turn bad sooner than we think possible. Higher temperatures enable many harmful organisms to multiply rapidly. Therefore it is absolutely necessary to inspect the cage, preferably every day, and to observe extreme cleanliness. It is also important that those birds living indoors for the greater part of the year, are taken outside at intervals—the more the better—during the spring and summer months. Do not place the cage in full sunshine however, but in a shady environment out of reach of cats, dogs and other predators. If you own cats, constant vigilance is vital. Many a cat has made victims of a fancier's birds, and if you are not careful your bird may meet this fate. While keeping an eye on the cage, it is sensible to place the cage without the metal or plastic tub-bottom on the grass, where the birds may walk about at will; in the afternoon you hay hose down the grass, providing it is a really warm summer day.

The Aviary

There are various possibilities, as far as aviaries are concerned. Some are illustrated in this book, but all have certain guidelines, which should be followed.

We distinguish between an inside and an outside aviary, which together form an ideal home for all parrot species. The sizes of aviaries will vary depending on the species being housed. For example, a couple of Blue-fronted Amazon Parrots or Macaws will require rather more space than a couple of Blue-crowned Hanging Parrots or Peach-faced Lovebirds.

Most aviaries consist of two or sometimes three parts: a night shelter, a

A view of some of the author's aviaries. *Vriends*

A simply constructed aviary such as the one shown here can be just as comfortable for the birds and enjoyable for the aviculturist as more elaborate arrangements. *Vriends*

This garden aviary has been designed and equipped for the maximum comfort of all the birds housed within it. *Kers*

41

half-open part (with the top covered by a sheet of corrugated fiberglass or similar material) and an open area which is called the flight. An aviary consisting of just two parts would lack the covered section of the flight.

An aviary consisting of three parts is, in my opinion, the most effective. If you can now choose a good location for your aviary, you will already be well along on the road to successful bird keeping.

An important requirement of the location is that the front of the aviary face south, if at all possible. If this is completely out of the question, the front should face as near south as possible, favoring southeast rather than southwest. It is also advisable to use glass in constructing part of the front (not plate glass), and this is certainly necessary if the front does not face south. Apart from this one requirement with regard to the location of the aviary, you should also try to pick a pretty place, preferably where flowers, bushes and trees will frame the aviary, rather than having it standing alone looking rather forlorn with nothing around it. The whole idea is to create as natural an effect as possible.

If the aviary is to be constructed of wood, certain parts of the structure should be protected with metal strips against the tendency of many hooked-billed birds to gnaw.

Building and Furnishing an Aviary

Unless you tend to move often, it is not a good idea to build your aviary of wood alone. The foundation can be made of concrete, poured with the upright 2 x 4's, metal poles or T-iron already in place. Next build a low wall of bricks between 12 and 20 inches (30 and 50 cm) high. The floor of the night shelter should be built at this level and is best made of concrete or concrete tiles. In my opinion, this is the best floor for this section. Of course it can also be made of creosote-treated wooden planks, particularly if there is a good chance you may need to move the aviary. The rest of the aviary, including the roof, is best made from tongue-and-groove pine board. In addition, you will need the following materials: wire mesh, wire thread and roof covering (such as tiles, slate, plastic corrugated sheets and fiberglass; there is a wide selection to choose from. Any planks used should be narrow; the narrower the better, since these are less subject to warping. Use the common aviary wire mesh which is six-sided if you keep tropical finches and such; if you keep parrots and parakeets, the square welded type wire mesh which is available in various thicknesses is preferable. It is best to use wired glass or safety glass. A maintenance-free aluminum gutter is very useful but not absolutely necessary.

If the size of an enclosure for chickens or ducks is usually determined by the number of chickens or ducks one plans to keep, the size of an aviary is determined the other way around. First establish the amount of space available, then determine the size of the aviary and finally the number of birds it can comfortably house. Even then, you must constantly beware of over-population. Of course an aviary can house a number of birds, but if little

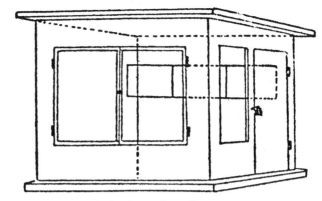

A simple, garden aviary.

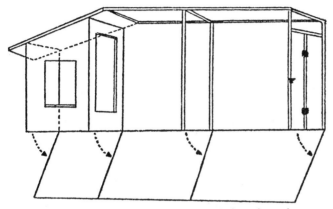

Another diagram for an easily-constructed garden aviary.

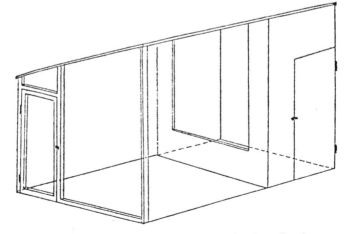

A garden aviary that is especially suited to breeding Lovebirds, Hanging Parrots and Lories.

43

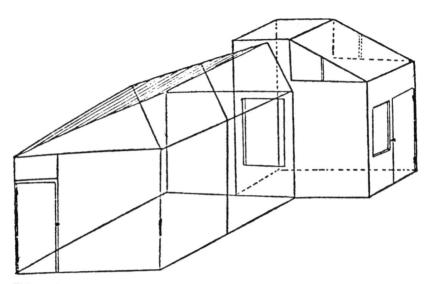

This garden aviary gives birds a little more space in the outdoor flight section as well as in the shelter.

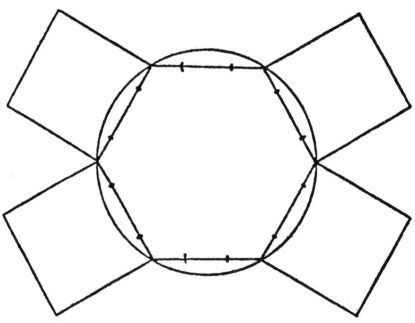

Four separate flights extend from a single, circular structure.

squabbles occur regularly, this indicates that your aviary is overpopulated. To start, select a compatible group of birds; not every bird can be placed with a given group! Peaceful co-existence is enhanced by species compatibility!

Keep the shape of the aviary straight and simple. The birds should be the focus of attention, not the domes, steeples and towers sometimes seen. Try to have the aviary's shape conform to the surroundings, both the ground plan and the enclosure itself. Again, the whole should fit in as smoothly as possible with the little piece of Nature you created. If you have no location that already meets these requirements, you will have to make the adjustments yourself by attractive, natural plantings.

Do not build your aviary too low. The front height should be a minimum of six or seven feet (two to 2½ meters) to achieve a good esthetic result.

Most parrots kept in the aviary can stay outdoors during the winter as well, providing they have good protection against wind and rain, and access to a draft-free night shelter. A completely open section of the aviary is also quite essential—you might take note of how many parrots will remain in this part of the aviary enjoying a reasonably heavy shower. In this completely open section, then, the walls and top are made of wire mesh. The floor should be made of sand so that a natural effect is achieved by installing several plants and shrubs, although your parrots' gnawing beaks will destroy these in no time at all. Hence *plant hardy shrubs* and *small trees* to provide plenty of shade.

Although a natural earth floor has many advantages, a cement or concrete floor is the better choice if you wish to keep and breed psittacines. On this floor, place large pots containing plants or arrange to pour the concrete to reserve several choice spots for planting shrubs. A cement floor can be hosed off daily, ridding it of any droppings and other dirt the birds have made, or the floor could be sprinkled with sand and grit which is replaced every two weeks. Part of the floor could be planted with sod; many birds very much enjoy frolicking on grass moist with dew or under the gentle spray of a garden hose. If you find it impossible to keep the sod alive, place it in low wooden boxes that can be removed whenever you wish to check or replace them without upsetting the birds.

The covered portion of the aviary has a watertight roof (preferably of sheet corrugated fiberglass or plastic, to transmit light), perhaps a back wall made of planking or concrete bricks, although fiberglass would do just as well, and the rest is made of wire mesh. The dividing wall can be built to be removable, separating the completely open area from the covered part of the flight. You might wish to put this divider, also made of mesh, into place in extended periods of bad weather. Some fanciers even make the wall of the completely closed area (which adjoins the flight) of mesh. Personally, I am not in favor of this, because I feel it does not afford enough protection against the elements; and it also means you cannot provide heat in the night shelter, should this ever be desirable, since, with one wall made of mesh, that would now be senseless.

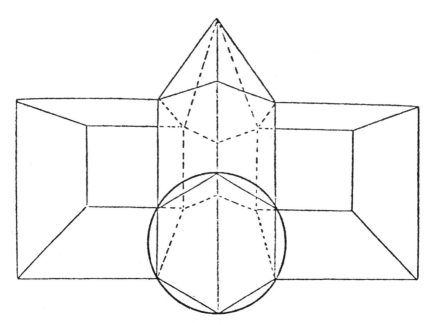

In this luxurious, outdoor aviary the roost is tower-shaped while the floor is an even hexagon. This diagram shows the hexagon in solid lines in projection and in dotted lines at floor level. There is an outdoor flight extending from either side of the central shelter.

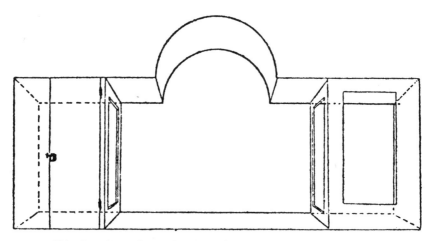

This elegant, outdoor aviary is equipped with two night shelters.

The floor of the covered section can also be of sand, or preferably, concrete, and by spraying aviary plants regularly, you remove the worry that these plants will not do very well. If you prefer a floor constructed of cement tiles, this is also perfectly acceptable. Such a floor, however, should be generously covered with coarse sand, in which the birds really enjoy picking and sand bathing. With such a floor, the natural growth would consist of one or more lovely dead trees, supplemented with artificial perches, and live plants, placed in pots and tubs. Unfortunately, this does little to help create the natural effect that we are trying so hard to achieve.

The night shelter is a little more complicated. First, at the front of the aviary, build a small safety room. This is to prevent the escape of birds and is absolutely essential. In this little entry room, then, there are no birds. There are five doors leading from it: 1) outer door; 2) door to covered section; 3) door to storage area; 4) door to the flight; 5) door to the night shelter.

Once in the little entry way, of course, close the door behind you to prevent the escape of any birds. Only then should you open the inner door leading to the flight. The next compartment is divided in half horizontally; the top half is the actual night shelter. The bottom half is split once more, this time vertically; one part is used for a mating room, quarantine station, punishment room for trouble makers, observation room, etc., while the other part is used for storing nesting boxes, perches, water and food containers, etc. The

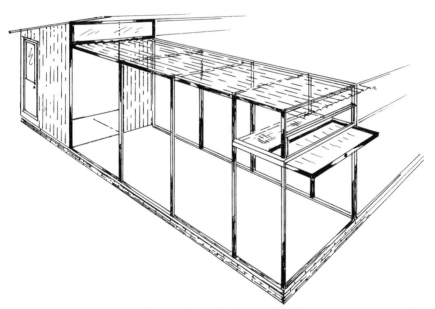

An aviary for Lories and Lorikeets. The platform at the right is where the birds are fed their special diet.

floor of both bottom halves can best be made of asbestos, concrete or tiles; the floor of the actual night shelter should also be made of concrete but covered with a layer of about 3 inches of coarse sand mixed with shell sand. The sides of the night shelter are made of safety glass; the division separating this part from the covered area could be made of wire if desired. The same applies to the inner aviary.

A few more important comments on the building of the aviary are necessary before moving on to other types of bird housing. When pouring the foundation, be sure to bury the wire mesh about 8 inches (20 cm) into the earth to deter rats and mice from entering the bird housing. It is also important to place wire in position when pouring the concrete to prevent it from cracking. The sides can be built using vertical tongue-and-groove boards. All windows, doors, etc. should be properly hung and should close tightly. To avoid puddles and the consequent rotting of materials, make sure the roof is built on a slant and extends on all sides. Naturally, the roof should be completely water-proof. The final touches consist of thoroughly staining all parts of the aviary—in fact, to help prevent the warping of the wood, you should treat all the wood with stain before you even begin the aviary! Even the wire should be given a coat of stain (use an almost dry brush) which also helps to make the birds a good deal more visible. The night shelter should not be painted, but it can be whitewashed, as long as this whitewash contains no harmful elements for whitewashes sooner or later will begin to peel. Pieces that are then picked up by the birds can be harmful to their health. If you wish to paint the inside, use child-safe paints (used for children's furniture) since these paints do not contain any harmful ingredients.

Salvadori's Lory (Lorius lory erythro-thoras)

48

The Bird Room

This is simply an outside aviary brought indoors. An attic, basement or other available room in the house will make an admirable bird room. The "building" of the bird room consists merely of fitting wire screens over the windows and building a little "porch" to prevent the birds from escaping, by means of an extra wire door. The rest of the setup is the same as for the outside aviary. The bird room is used a great deal for breeding Lovebirds and other small parrots. A bird room is also very suitable for keeping the more exotic species (Lories and Lorikeets), particularly those birds that cannot tolerate temperate or cold climate very well, and do better in a climate-controlled aviary. Very expensive species are often kept this way. Bird rooms are often used by more experienced fanciers, but the beginning bird enthusiast can also achieve successful breeding results in a bird room.

Always try to achieve a natural effect; the floor consists of tiles upon which is placed a layer of beach sand, which of course must be refreshed regularly; on top of the beach sand is a layer of coarse sand and grit. Try also to maintain as much natural shrubbery as possible, although of course these must be placed in tubs and pots.

With a little artistic insight and imagination, you can create a beautiful piece of Nature right inside your own home!

The Indoor Aviary

The indoor aviary can best be described as follows: it is a small aviary placed in some room of the house or in an attic, around which are grouped arrangements of plants and in which are placed a few colorful, small psittacines. The setup is again the same as in an outside aviary.

Many people confuse an indoor aviary with a bird room. A bird room, however, is always an entire room set up only to house birds, not used for anything else by the residents of the house; the indoor aviary is an aviary placed in a room where other activity takes place.

The indoor aviary is currently very popular; there are even a few manufacturers that make some ready-made models, and these certainly meet the necessary requirements. I have seen some indoor aviaries that were truly beautiful and in which successful breeding results were regularly achieved. The bird population seemed to be unconcerned by the children playing nearby on the floor.

I prefer not to delve into the details regarding glass enclosures and other small types of bird housing, since these are already very well-known. Glass enclosures or vitrines are usually a closed type of bird housing with only the front and top made of wire. Through the use of an abundant amount of shrubbery and effective lighting, a fairy tale effect can be achieved that is as enchanting as it is colorful. It is best to keep just one pair of small parrots (Lovebirds, Dwarf Parrots, Lories, etc.), and if nest boxes are made available, they will often breed.

49

Perches In the Aviary

Perches should be made of hardwood like those used in cages. Provide your birds with twigs and small branches from fruit trees so they can aim their gnawing attacks on these rather than at the perches. Another advantage of providing twigs for gnawing is that your birds won't start the bad habit of pecking at each other's feathers. Affix the perches at both ends of the flight so they do not interfere with the length of the flight available to the birds. Perches should not be installed too close to the wire, however, both because of cats, which can pose a definite danger, and because the birds' tail feathers will eventually become frayed if they are constantly rubbed against the wire. If you can place an old tree trunk in the center of the aviary or build the aviary around one, by all means do so.

Bathing Facilities In the Aviary

Every aviary should be equipped with flat ceramic saucers allowing the birds to bathe. On colder days, of course, remove these dishes. Make sure that your birds are dry before they go to sleep; that is, they should not have the opportunity to bathe after four or five p.m. You could also put a garden sprinkler to good use, as many birds prefer a gentle shower to a tub bath. Ponds with rocks and running water are obviously idyllic, but unfortunately not something that everyone can afford. Perches, of course, should not be situated above any of these bathing or drinking facilities. The water in the saucers should be changed daily.

Water and Seed Dishes In the Aviary

Directions in the feeding chapter pertain to both the fancier who keeps one bird in a cage and the fancier who maintains several aviaries. However, one must realize that a bird living in an aviary has a great deal more room for flying and hence gets a lot more exercise. Consequently, seeds containing fats, such as hemp, sunflower, linseed, maw, rape and peanuts can be given in greater quantities. Use indestructible seed feeders that are easily cleaned and made so the parrots cannot soil the contents in any way and cannot sit or walk on seeds. Wooden feeders, of course, would soon be reduced to splinters. There are several feeders on the market, and local pet shop staff can advise you on them. Saucers made of glass, ceramic, and such are suitable as well and are most often used both for seed and for water.

The most practical feeders, however, are the box-like hoppers with glass fronts called self-feeders. These hoppers usually hold quantities of seed sufficient for a number of days. They are often divided into a few narrow compartments in which each kind of seed is given separately, enabling the birds to make their own mixture to suit their needs. Around the bottom of these feeders a detachable tray extends that is designed to catch seeds thrown aside by the parrots.

50

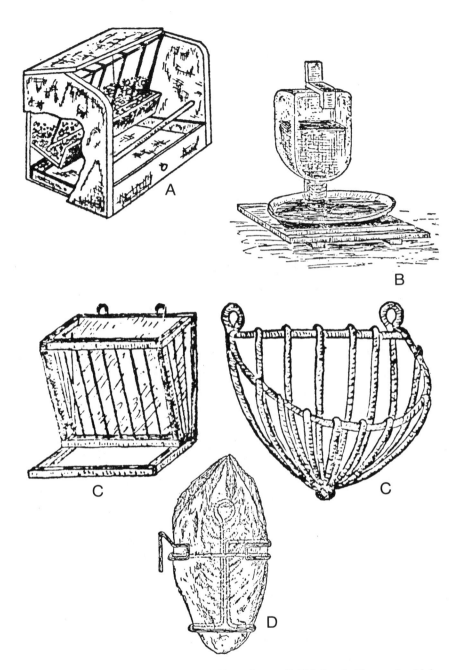

A. An automatic seed tray fitted with a spillage drawer. B. This bowl will serve for drinking or bathing. The water source is an old ink-bottle. C. These racks are used for supplying green food without risk of contamination from cage or aviary floor and, for some species, nesting material. D. Cuttlebone supplies essential minerals to all psittacines. The wire holder can be made or purchased.

Three Long-billed Corellas sharing a perch with a young Galah.
Sloots

A pair of Galahs at a possible nesting site. Here the male is making a closer inspection.
Kers

Maintenance

The sand sprinkled on the aviary floor must be replaced regularly, while the soil will need to be dug up on a regular basis, the frequency depending upon the size of the aviary and the number of inhabitants. At least once every spring all perches should be cleaned and disinfected. All shrubbery and any other natural perches must be pruned whenever necessary and any rotten or dying pieces removed from the aviary. All woodwork and metal in the aviary must be hosed off, and any dead plants should be replaced.

If at all possible, house your birds in flight cages temporarily during cleaning operations. This gives you the opportunity to really clean both the interior and exterior, and repair any leaks, drafts, faults in the wire, locks or whatever, and bring everything back into top form. Should you decide to winter your birds indoors, including winter-hardened birds that could spend the winter outside, this would be the ideal time to check and repair everything at your leisure. By repeating this procedure each year, it is most unlikely that you will be surprised by a great many problems at any one time. During the winter, when there is no breeding activity anyway, be sure to do a thorough cleaning job on the nesting boxes, because these in particular are favorite breeding grounds of bacteria. Thus disease could easily develop a stronghold here. Besides these nesting boxes, don't overlook feed hoppers, water dishes, fountains and birdbaths. The feed and water hoppers should be placed in such a way that the bird fancier has easy access to them without disturbing his birds too much. During the breeding season in particular it is desirable to give birds as much peace and quiet as possible so they can watch their eggs or young virtually undisturbed.

Keep your aviary as clean as you can . . . both you and your birds will benefit!

Because of the particular arrangement of the toes on psittacine species, these birds have the ability to hold their food in one foot while eating. This trait is common to all genera and is here demonstrated with an Illiger's Macaw (a New World species) above left and an African Grey (an Old World species) below.   *Vriends   Leysen/Vriends*

54

3

Food and
Drinking Water

BY CONSISTENTLY PROVIDING certain basic requirements, the pet owner will probably never face many unpleasant surprises concerning his bird's housing, care and food. First, birds must be suitably housed, and every day, regardless of housing arrangements, your birds' drinking water must be freshened. In large aviaries with many inhabitants, it is essential to freshen their water several times daily. The bottom of a parrot cage must be cleaned and recovered with pure sand twice a week, preferably at a set time. The perches should be sanded clean and disinfected at least once weekly. They can also use more frequent cleanings, particularly in the spring and summer months. Drinking water and perches are often ideal breeding places for bacteria so that extra attention to their cleanliness is highly desirable. The glass or plastic around the cage should also be cleaned twice a week, either with a sponge and chamois cloth, or glass cleaner applied on a paper towel.

Aviaries and other types of bird housing for larger populations are also subject to weekly cleaning. The water and seed dishes should be cleaned at least every day; the night shelter must be checked weekly for harmful insects, which, if spotted, must be exterminated. Any openings in the night shelter or the nesting boxes can be the daytime refuge for bird lice and other pests. Run the blade of a pocket knife between the wood joints; if there is any sign of blood on the blade, your aviary has been invaded by these pesky parasites. Spray with bird sprays available in your pet shop, and don't forget all cracks and crevices!

Birds should have access to fresh bath water every day, weather permitting; it will be enthusiastically used by many species. Later in this chapter, water will be considered in greater detail.

Talking About Food

Psittacines are seed-eaters, as evidenced by their sturdy beaks! Their vegetarian diet, then, must include all the elements such birds need: protein, fat, carbohydrates, vitamins, calcium, and trace elements. No single seed possesses all of those nutrients, so several different seed varieties are used in varying quantities to form a seed mixture providing complete nutrition. There are several excellent pre-mixed seed varieties available on the market which have become world famous, and for good reason. Before going into more detail, I must point out that the value of the seed is determined by, among other factors, sunlight and humidity, as well as soil condition and quality. Take the well-known canary seed as an example. Scientifically known as *Phalaris canariensis,* canary seed will be gratefully accepted by your Canaries, Budgerigars, Lovebirds and many other small parrots and parakeets; even African Greys like it. Although some canary seed is grown locally, most of this elongated seed comes from Argentina, Morocco, and Australia. Three different sources immediately implies three different qualities in form, color, and food value. The various canary seed types can be purchased individually, but should then be bought on an alternating basis, this presuming of course that you mix the seed varieties yourself. Again, there are very good pre-mixed brands available offering consistent quality and ratio based on scientific tests, thus eliminating potentially harmful guesswork.

Protein is the most important food element, since it helps to maintain and build up the bird's body. The unhatched chick starts its existence feeding upon egg white, a proteinaceous substance which is found in large quantities in a bird's egg. It would follow that an adult bird also must have protein on a daily basis. If protein is missing or given in insufficient amounts, it will soon become apparent by the bird's deteriorating condition. Therefore a good, well-balanced bird menu is rich in protein. In fact, it has been determined that a large percentage of a psittacine's daily food intake should consist of protein. You achieve this goal by offering protein-rich seed varieties as your birds' "main dish," such as given in this table:

Seed	Protein calories/gram	Seed	Protein calories/gram
Canary	15.1	Maw	17.0
White millet	11.0	Niger	20.7
Yellow millet	11.1	Rape	20.0
Oats	10.4	Linseed	21.5
Hemp	19.5	Wheat	11.5
Sunflower	27.7	Corn	9.1

This average is taken from various analyses. The methods vary somewhat and give slightly different results. Different samples of seeds, too, vary.

Protein consists primarily of amino acids and is an essential food element in the diet, particularly for the formation of the new protoplasm for cells, of which the parrot's body (and every living thing) is built. Protein possesses the following chemical elements: carbon, hydrogen, oxygen, nitrogen, and usually a small amount of sulphur, as well as a few other elements, depending upon the source.

This summary will clarify why protein is so essential for the growth, repair, and replacement of "worn out" parts of the body. In addition to all these functions, it also generates energy through oxidation. Since protein cannot be stored by the body, it is necessary that it be available daily. If the body consumes too much protein, it will be converted into glycogen, an insoluble carbohydrate stored in the liver. Protein appears in large quantities in meat, as an example, which explains why psittacines will eat insects or their direct replacements; therefore we offer them universal food and rearing food which contains eggs (an animal product), among other foods. Milk also contains protein, and a slice of bread soaked in milk will generally be eaten by most birds. Here again, we could substitute rusk crumbs, cookies or bread. There are even a few companies that make rusk flour (so-called egg rusks) from which we can make our own chick rearing and strength foods.

Carbohydrates also play an important role in the diet (see the table below). Carbohydrates contain carbon, oxygen, and hydrogen and are found in the form of starches and sugar. Carbohydrates are found in white and yellow millet, oats, wheat and corn. Canary seed also contains a high percentage of carbohydrates. Starch is really a form of sugar. Since sugar can be directly absorbed by the body (starch is first broken down into molecules through chemicals found in saliva), it can enter the bloodstream via the small intestine and then be transported to the tissues. At that point it can be considered energy; in other words, as carbohydrates are burned, they supply warmth and energy. This brings us to the next fact: every gram of carbohydrates supplies 4.1 kilocalories of energy. It is interesting to know that an overabundance of carbohydrates in mammals is stored in the muscles and liver in the form of glycogen, or can be converted into fat and stored under the skin. This process can be clearly observed with animals that spend a part of the year in particularly cold regions.

The function of fats is more or less the same as carbohydrates. Fats contain carbon, hydrogen, and oxygen, but of course in different ratios than carbohydrates. Among other sources, fats can be found in milk, animal fat, and egg yolks. Fat is fuel for energy and warmth, though we should keep in mind that it is considerably more difficult for the body to digest and absorb fats than carbohydrates. On the other hand, the caloric value of fat is twice as great. Important vitamins, such as A and D and the so-called "fertility vitamin", E, can be found dissolved in fats. As digestion of fat is slower than that of carbohydrates, our parrots can go much longer on fats. This certainly has its advantage in winter when the nights are long and cold, and there are fewer daylight hours, which would tend to decrease the amount of food consumed. Parrots have a greater need for seeds with a higher fat content during the fall and winter months. The following table is intended to give you some idea of the content of various seeds with regard to protein, carbohydrates, and fat.

Seed	Protein calories/gram	Carbohydrates calories/gram	Fats calories/gram
Buckwheat	11.5	57.8	2.4
Canary	15.1	56.0	6.1
Corn	9.1	69.8	4.2
Hemp	19.5	18.0	32.1
Linseed	21.5	22.3	34.2
Millet	11.1	59.8	3.7
Niger	20.7	13.1	42.2
Oats	10.4	59.7	4.9
Rape	20.0	17.8	42.6
Rice	7.7	77.0	1.1
Rice (paddy)	7.1	64.1	2.1
Sorghum-dari	10.2	69.6	3.2
Sunflower	27.7	13.1	45.2
Wheat	11.5	68.8	1.7

These figures should help you choose the right seed for each season!

Calcium and trace elements are found in mineral salts, of which there are a great variety. These salts and others are absolutely necessary for the chemical activities inside the bird's body and for building certain tissues. As examples, the red coloring in the blood (hemoglobin) contains iron, the skeleton contains calcium, magnesium, and phosphorus, and almost all cells, nerves, and body fluids cannot do without sodium and potassium. In man iodine is imperative to insure the proper functioning of the thyroid. Besides nitrogen and sulphur in the proteins, traces of copper, cobalt and manganese can also be found, which are all essential. If we study calcium in a little more detail, we will all agree that calcium (particularly calcium phosphate) is tremendously important for the bird egg, which has a shell of calcium, as well as the skeleton of the chick. There is no need to worry about trace elements because the salts of these elements are present in normal food, though in very small amounts, so the body can absorb and concentrate them. If you feed a well-balanced menu, your parrots will not suffer any deficiencies of iron, potassium, magnesium, and other elements.

On vitamins, articles in bird magazines make frequent mention of the importance of offering food rich in vitamins to our feathered friends. Vitamins cause rather complicated chemical reactions which are essential to the normal metabolic processes in the broadest sense, though they have no bearing on the generation of energy. If there is any lack of certain vitamins in the diet, the normal process of chemical reactions will be affected, with the

A group of 5½ week-old, hand raised Sulphur-crested Cockatoos is unanimous in the idea that "anytime is dinnertime!" The bird at left against the wall is first at the spoon. *Sloots*

A magnificent Green-winged Macaw *(Ara chloroptera)* extends the hospitality of his feeding tray to a neighboring squirrel. *Vriends*

appearance of corresponding disease symptoms as a result. Consequently, the simplest and most effective cure is to bring the diet back up to the required standards and make up for the deficiency by giving supplementary doses of the vitamin in question. If a particular vitamin cannot be found in the diet you are giving your parrots or the amount present is too small, supplement with vitamin preparations (obtainable in every good pet shop). Usually a few drops mixed in with universal or chick rearing food will bring about a rapid improvement. Since animals—including parrots—cannot manufacture most of their own vitamins from simple elements as plants can, they will have to absorb their vitamins ready-made, through the (direct or indirect) consumption of plants.

At the moment, man has isolated over fifteen different vitamins. The most important ones to us as bird fanciers are vitamins A, B, C, D and E; there are also twelve different varieties of vitamin B. For example, the source of vitamin B_1 is wheat germ and yeast, while B_2 is found in yeast, milk and vegetables. B vitamins are a very important group because they have an influence on the proper digestion of carbohydrates, stimulate growth, and prevent anemia. A bird can manufacture its own vitamin C if the diet includes sufficient vegetables and some fruits or fruit substitutes, such as a few drops of orange juice mixed in with universal or chick rearing food. It is unlikely that your parrots will be deficient in the very important vitamin C, providing we follow this regimen. The importance of vitamin C lies in the fact that it provides birds with an excellent resistance to disease and aids the speedy healing of small wounds.

Thanks to sunlight, vitamin D can also be formed inside the bird's body. Vitamin D can be found in cod-liver oil and egg yolks, with cream and milk as important sources. This vitamin is also essential to the proper development of the skeleton; rachitis (commonly known as rickets) is the result of a deficiency in vitamin D.

In order to furnish a menu rich in vitamins, be sure to give your birds fresh seeds, fresh greens, sprouted seeds, half-ripe weed seeds, and fruit. If parrots are provided with the proper diet, I advise against supplementing with extra vitamin preparations or wheat germ oil. The latter is sometimes fed during the breeding season, since it contains vitamin E and is therefore said to promote the fertility. Personally, I feel that wheat germ oil need not be given to our birds as long as they are offered fresh greens and sprouted seed varieties on a daily basis. I do think it is advisable to mix a few drops of cod-liver oil in with the seeds during the winter months. If you use 1½ drops per pound of seed, the risk of vitamin deficiencies is greatly reduced. Of course this assumes that you give your birds sprouted seeds and greens throughout the year as well. Make sure that the seeds are fresh, because old seeds lose a great deal of their nutritional value. This is why it is so important to obtain the seed supply from a trusted source. Never buy a seed supply to last longer than a few months, and make it a point to regularly check the purchased seeds to see if they will still germinate. Sprinkle a few seeds on a flat plate and pour a little lukewarm water on the seeds. Leave them for one day, preferably in a warm location. The second day rinse the seeds and again cover them with lukewarm water. If after four days there is still no sign of germination, the seeds are old and you might consider a new source of supply.

Water

A large percentage of any animal's body consists of water. Water is the essential element in the normal protoplasm in the cell, where the chemical processes take place that are so important to life. Water plays an important role in the digestion of food and in the transportation of nutrients; all chemical reactions in the body can take place only in a solution containing water. This is why water is so important in the diet. Consequently, birds must have daily access to pure, fresh water. A biological and chemical examination of a recently deceased bird would reveal that its body is made up of over 75% water, and this is only considering the tissues! If you serve your birds impure water, the chances of their becoming ill are great. Intestinal disorders are among the least of the problems to expect! An ideal drinking water supply—if you could make it—would be some kind of waterfall with water streaming over rocks and a drainage gutter carrying the water out of the aviary. This could be costly, but if many birds are involved it might be worth the effort and the difference in price over the common earthenware drinking dishes and other conventional watering systems. Those dishes are open, of course, and therefore not very hygienic, not only because many birds like to bathe in them, but because dust and other impurities find their way into them. Fountains and automatic waterers may be subject to the same risks but to a lesser extent, because they fill up by themselves and their size is such that parrots are not as tempted to bathe in them. If your birds stay outdoors during the winter, wire or asbestos slats should be placed over the bowls because birds like to bathe no matter what the weather if given the opportunity. The results of bathing in cold weather can be disastrous.

In breeding cages, display cages, and other small enclosures, provide water in glass, porcelain or plastic containers. These are not only easy to clean, but because they are small, you must fill them with fresh water regularly. You can often observe the growth of algae in water containers. This can be quite difficult to remove in closed water bottles, but if you place a few bicycle ball-bearings in the bottle while cleaning it, you will be amazed how quickly algae disappears.

Water, then, must always be present, in winter and all year 'round. It must be clean and will need to be replaced more often on some days than others. Regular tap water is fine, although some parrots and parakeets are leery of the fluoride and chlorine added to most water supplies. Although it has not been proved that either of these elements is damaging to birds, rain-water, filtered through a closely-woven linen cloth or charcoal, is ideal and is especially recommended during the breeding season.

Dissolving a few grains of iodized salt in the drinking water supplies birds with the small amount of iodine required in their diet. Parrot fanciers who have convenient access to seawater should certainly use this as drinking water for their birds, no matter how strange it may sound. Seawater contains practically all the minerals that a parrot needs, lacking only calcium. Offer only pure seawater (an item becoming more difficult to provide with each passing day, alas) in a separate dish and replace it daily. Of course most seawater in undiluted form is much too salty for all but sea birds. The best results come from using one teaspoon of seawater to a cup of tapwater. This same solution can be used when soaking seeds. In this manner your parrots will get all but one of the necessary minerals. Never soak more seeds than will be consumed in one day, however.

Coprophagy

When I stated earlier that calcium cannot be found in seawater, I was reminded of the bird fancier who swore up and down that birds have no great need of calcium. Previous pages should have proven otherwise. A calcium deficiency can also cause birds to start pecking at their own droppings and eating them! Naturally, you'll want to put an immediate stop to this distasteful coprophagy habit. First, you must change the seed mixture; as you know, calcium can be found in seed. Also try to get your birds to gnaw at cuttlebone and grit. There are also mineral blocks available on the market which are excellent. Although it was previously thought that birds in captivity only needed minerals during the molting period, studies have definitely proved that parrots require minerals at all times. If your birds are not touching the cuttlebone or the mineral blocks, crumble and mix them in with the seed or place them on the floor of the aviary or cage. Only do this, however, if the birds indicate a total lack of interest, as gnawing on whole mineral blocks and cuttlebone will help keep the beak in proper shape.

Weeds

Although wild birds will instinctively not eat poisonous plants, this is not necessarily true of birds that have been domesticated for centuries. Further studies, however, have yet to be made on this subject. The assumption that Amazons, Budgerigars, Lovebirds and others will avoid all poisonous weeds is still in question. Therefore, it would seem logical to take the safe route and only make available those plants which can be definitely identified. A simple guidebook to assist in making these identifications, preferably one with clear illustrations, is well worth the nominal investment. *Weeds, A Golden Nature Guide* published by Western Publishing Co., is a small, inexpensive book that will make child's play out of identifying common yard and field plants. Several other titles should be available at your local bookstore.

A word of warning with regard to searching for weeds: as you know, insecticides are widely used in orchards, along highways, on land used for agriculture. Plants that have been sprayed with an insecticide are extremely dangerous to birds. When looking for weeds, be sure you can observe insects flying about. If everything is too quiet, it would be wise to find a different location for your weed source. Of course, most of you will probably have no shortage of weeds right in your own garden! Even window flower boxes might produce a few weeds. In this event we can really be sure that they have not been sprayed. Store weed seeds in a dry, cool place, and you can provide them for your birds even during the winter months.

The following plants would be suitable:

Hedge nettle (*Stachys arvensis*)

Canada thistle (*Cirsium arvense*)

Perennial sow thistle (*Sonchus arvensis*)

Rabbitsfood grass (*Polypogon monspeliensis*)

Mugwort (*Artemisia vulgaris*)

Chicory (*Cichoram intybus*); the cultivated form is known as *Chichoram sativum*

Spanish needles, sticktights (various species of the genus *Bidens*)

Yarrow (*Archillea millefolium*)

Snowball, high-bush cranberry (*Viburnum opulus*)

Goldenrods (various species of the genus *Solidago*)

Meadow salsify (*Tragopogon pratensis*)

Hemp nettle (*Galeopsis tetrahit*)

Wild mustard (*Brassica arvensis*)

Falseflax (*Camelina sativa*)

Knapweed (*Centaurea jacea*)

Common groundel (*Senecio vulgaris*)

Common chickweed (*Stellaria media*); there are several varieties. This is the ideal green food for practically all our birds!

Stitchwort (*Stellaria graminea*)

Dock or sorrel (*Rumex obtusifolius*); the species *Rumex acetosa,* common sorrel, is probably the most suitable of all the dock species!

Kentucky blue grass (*Poa pratensis*)

Spear grass (*Poa annua*)

Plantains (family *Plantaginaceae*) have basal rosette of large leaves and small greenish flowers in spikes. Broadleaf plantain (*Plantago major*) is used a great deal. The leaves are weakly covered with hair or are smooth. The leaves are attached by long stems. The dense, narrow spike of small yellowish white flowers has anthers that are first a purple shade and later turn white. It blooms from May into the fall and is very common practically everywhere. Height: to 18 inches (45 cm). Buckhorn plaintain (*P. lanceolata*) has a thick root with many runners. The oval or lancet-shaped leaves are quite pointy. It has yellowish anthers, is very common, and blooms from April to late into the fall. Height: to 18 inches (45 cm). *Plantago media* has leaves attached to short stems and with a dense covering of hair. The anthers are lilac. It is common along rivers and on lime-rich soil, but can also be found along highways. It blooms from May to August. *Plantago coronopus* has leaves arranged in a basal rosette; they are generally deeply indented. The anthers are yellowish white. This plant is particularly common along the seashore and blooms from May to October.

Needless to say, there are many more weeds that could be suitable as "greens" or for their seeds. I stress the fact that to achieve successful breeding results, weed and grass seeds are an absolute must. Keep in mind, however, that towns and many farmers do a great deal of spraying with insecticides. Any insecticide is dangerous to your birds, so be alert!

Sprouted Seed

Sprouted seeds are always welcome, but especially just before and during the breeding period. It is best to use rape seed, niger seed, the seeds mentioned above, or you could purchase the special assortment of sprouted seed mixes available at any good seed supply store. Use a smooth, not too thin cloth and moisten it with lukewarm water. Spread the cloth out on a flat plate or a cookie sheet. Sprinkle the seeds onto the cloth and place the whole thing in a warm, humid location. When the seeds burst open, rinse them off with a little water, using a strainer, and serve them to parrots and parakeets in a separate dish. Do not give more than your birds can consume in one day, and throw out whatever is left at night. Seed that has gone sour will only cause problems, such as intestinal upsets. Weed seeds can be used in the above manner, too. Further, it does not take a great deal of effort to plant some weed seeds on the soil floor of the aviary; sprouting seeds and seedlings are much enjoyed by your birds. In fact, you need not remove seed that the birds have spilled from the feeder; these may develop into a little green corner where your birds will gratefully "nose around" looking for seedlings.

Chickrearing and Strength Foods

Chickrearing food is actually a kind of egg food and can be bought under several widely-known names. Chickrearing food, as the name implies, is essential during the breeding period. It often happens that breeders switch to a different brand, particularly in the breeding season, because they feel that their mediocre results of the previous season(s) were due to the brand they were then using. Usually, however, there are other reasons for unsuccessful clutches. Keep in mind that every brand available has a great deal of research behind it and that competition is much too fierce to give an inferior brand much of a chance to survive. If you still feel that you will have better results with a different brand than the one you are currently using (perhaps because at a club meeting you heard someone bragging about the fantastic results he achieved using a particular brand of food), then of course go ahead and change brands. Never do this, however, during the breeding season; allow

Eclectus Parrots (*Eclectus roratus*) are highly prized in aviculture for their exquisite color and gentle disposition. The female is shown in the foreground, the male in the rear.   *Leysen*

Peach-faced Lovebirds (*Agapornis roseicollis*) are one of the most familiar of all Lovebird species.   *Ebben*

The Citron-crested Cockatoo (*Cacatua sulphurea citrinocristata*) is a subspecies of the Lesser Sulphur-crested Cockatoo. It is distinguished chiefly by its bright orange crest.　*Leysen*

The Lesser Sulphur-crested Cockatoo (*Cacatua sulphurea*) was first described in the latter half of the 18th century and is held in the highest esteem by bird fanciers all over the world. *Ebben*

66

The Long-billed Corella *(Cacatua tenuirostris)* is native to south-eastern Australia and shows a natural adaptation for gathering roots and other food matter. The specialized beak is an excellent tool for digging and foraging on the ground. A friendly, if noisy, bird, it is becoming increasingly rare in the wild, but is very popular as a pet in Australia and New Zealand. *Leysen*

The Hyacinth Macaw (*Anodorhynchus hyacinthinus*) is one of the most spectacular of all psittacines. Its great size, sensuous coloring and other physical attributes all contribute to the regal picture it makes. A native of southern Brazil, it is a highly prized addition to any collection of exotic birds. *Leysen*

The Blue and Gold Macaw *(Ara ararauna)* is another familiar species that has been known outside its natural range for many years. This beautiful bird is widely distributed in Central and South America attesting to its ability to adapt. *Leysen*

The Scarlet Macaw (Ara macao) is probably the most familiar member of his family. His commanding size, resplendent coloration and bold manner render him instantly recognizable to almost any bird lover. *Leysen*

The Military Macaw (Ara militaris) does not boast the brilliant coloration of some other Macaw species, but has many positive attributes to recommend it to any bird enthusiast. *Leysen*

69

The Red-fronted Macaw *(Ara rubrogenys)* is one of the great rarities of the parrot family, due in large part to a very severely restricted natural habitat.   *Lesyen*

Illiger's Macaw *(Ara maracana)* is one of the several "dwarf" species. Similar to the Severe Macaw, Illiger's is particularly fond of water and loves a good romp in the trees on a rainy day — the rainier the better.
Leysen

Rare, bizarre, intriguing are all apt words to describe Pesquet's Parrot *(Psittrichas fulgidus),* a species some authorities think might bear physical similarities to an ancient psittacine form. Seldom seen even in the largest collections, these birds come from the more remote mountainous sections of New Guinea.

Leysen/Vriends

The Masked Lovebird *(Agapornis personata)*, like the Peach-faced, is one of the most familiar members of genus *Agapornis*. Both *A. personata* and *A. roseicollis* have produced interesting color mutations in captivity. *Vriends*

ample time before the breeding season starts so that your birds have the opportunity to become accustomed to their new food. Don't add all kinds of vitamins to these prepared foods, as an overdose may result in your birds becoming sick. Among older parrot breeders there are probably many who prefer to make their own mixtures of one hard-boiled egg and four rusks. I must admit that personal experience has shown that this mixture achieved very good results for the small parrot-like birds. Boil fresh eggs for ten minutes, and, if you feel so inclined, add a little lettuce and some maw seed as well as a little grated carrot and finely chopped chickweed. Do not use egg powder, as this can very easily cause constipation. It is very important that this mixture, too, must be made fresh daily.

I am sure you will understand that young, recently flighted birds must also have access to this egg food. Their switchover to regular seed mixtures must be gradual. Incidentally, a parrot in a cage will also greatly benefit from some chickrearing food from time to time.

Parrots should also be given some "strength foods" on a daily basis, though care should be taken that they do not overfeed themselves on this type of food. A good guide would be two teaspoons per day per small parrot; three per day for a bigger species. Lories and such birds require a different diet. It is unlikely, anyway, that they would eat more than this if given the opportunity. Should they go overboard with it on occasion, it's still not the end of the world! Parrots kept in a cage can empty a treat dish every other day.

Strength food is available in prepared form.

Greens

Greens must always be part of a bird's menu. The importance of greens was emphasized when I discussed weeds. A parrot in a cage should also be given some greens. At least every other day, and preferably daily, a parrot in a cage or an outdoor aviary should be offered lettuce, spinach, cabbage, endive, a piece of carrot, chickweed or other green food. The greens must be fresh, and any left over should be removed before your parrots go to sleep that night. To insure that you use safe, unsprayed vegetables, you could cultivate your own if you like. If you do, try growing spinach, carrots, lettuce, watercress, chicory and thistle.

Fruit

Many parrots and parakeets love fruit, such as apple, pear, tomato, pineapple, cherries, grapes, grapefruit, guavas, berries and bananas. Large pieces are best stuck onto a nail that has been hammered into a piece of wood so that the fruit won't become soiled on the aviary floor. You can also place pieces in special wire fruit holders. Their practicality seems somewhat obscure to me, though, since the fruit ends up falling through the wire sooner or later anyway.

73

A baby Blue and Gold Macaw raised by Mr. R. Keulen.   *Kers*

The same bird as above, a little older and much more developed in plumage.   *Kers*

Minerals

With a balanced diet it is unlikely that your birds will suffer from any mineral deficiencies. There are several mineral preparations that can be purchased, however. If your birds get enough minerals, late molt, egg binding, and other such discomforts will be rare. These prepared minerals need only be sprinkled on the floor of the aviary or cage, so it certainly does not require much effort. In this regard, when we use special bird charcoal it is best to place this in a separate little dish rather than on the floor, especially in an aviary or breeding cage. Charcoal is extremely helpful to the chemical reactions that take place within a bird's body.

Grit and Cuttlebone

Grit and cuttlebone are essential. Grit is important to the digestive system for grinding seeds in the crop and cuttlebone assists with the formation of calcium. Cuttlebone can be purchased complete with holder, and is reasonably priced. If you should have access to unprepared (natural) cuttlebones be sure to soak them for a few days first, because their salt content is too high for direct consumption by parrots. Cuttlebone is also very important during molting. It would be a good idea to always have some on hand so that our birds need never do without.

Daily Diets

I. PARROT SEED MIXTURE—½ ounce (15 g.) per day per parrot
Barley 5%
Buckwheat 5%
Canary 10%
Corn 15%
Eucalyptus seed 5%
Hemp 5%
Melaleuca seed (Gottlebrush bush) 5%
Millet 5%
Oats 5%
Paddy 10%
Sorghum 5%
Sunflower 15%
Wheat 10%

The above seed mixture can be used for African Greys, Amazon Parrots, Cockatoos, Eclectus Parrots, Hawk-Headed Parrots, Keas and Senegal Parrots.

All birds need, as an extra, corn on the cob (2%), banksia (2%) and pine (2%), although not all species will accept those seeds.

Lovebird Seed Mixture—½ ounce (15 g.) per day per parrot
Buckwheat 10%

Canary 20%
Hemp 5%
Millet 35%
Oats 10%
Paddy 10%
Sunflower 10%
(As an extra, daily millet spray)

II. NUTS—½ to ¾ ounce (15-20 g.) per day per parrot; in separate dish; a choice of:

Almonds
Brazil Nuts
Grated Coconut
Macadamia
Peanuts
Pine Nuts
Walnuts

(It is advisable to place one drop of wheat germ oil in the opened end of a peanut during the breeding season and at molting time)

The above nuts can be offered to Amazons, Macaws and Gang Gang Cockatoos. All other Cockatoo species like almonds and peanuts daily. African Greys, Pesquet's Parrots and Keas also relish peanuts and can take up to ¾ to 1 ounce (20-25 g.) per day per parrot.

III. FRUITS—1½ ounces (40 g.) per day per parrot; a choice of:

Apple (cut in pieces or quarters)
Banana (cut in pieces)
Berries
Cherries
Contoneaster Berries
Eugenia
Fresh Figs
Guava
Grapes
Grapefruit
Hawthorn
Mulberries
Orange (cut in pieces)
Pandamus Serew Pine (exclusively for the Great Black Cockatoo)
Papaya
Pineapple
Plums
Pyracantha
Tomato

76

Macaws: apple, banana and/or orange

Cockatoos: apple and/or orange

Gang Gang Cockatoo: contoneaster berries, eugenia, hawthorn, mulberries and pyracantha

Amazons: apple, banana, and/or orange

Eclectus Parrot: apple, banana, fresh figs, grapes, tomato, papaya and pears

Hawk-headed Parrot: banana, cherries, fresh figs, tomato, grapes

Pesquet's Parrot: figs, grapes (or guavas) and papaya

African Grey Parrot: apple, banana and orange

Senegal Parrot: apple, cherries, and plum

Blue-crowned or Philippine Racquet-tailed Parrot: blueberries, fresh figs, papaya and pear

Kea: apple

Loriculus species (Hanging Parrots): apple, fresh figs, papaya and pear— only ¼ ounce (6 g.) per day per bird

Lories and Lorikeets: apples and/or papaya on spikes, fresh figs (diced), pears, soaked (12 hours) raisins. Kenton C. Lint recommends canned fruit cocktail or diced fruits with ¼ ounce (5 g.) corn syrup added to a whole can of fruit.

IV. GREENS—¾ ounce (20 g.) per day per (large) species, like Cockatoos, Amazons and such. ½ ounce (15 g.) per day for smaller parrots, such as Lovebirds; a choice of:

Acacia blossoms
Calendula buds
Carrot tops
Chickweed
Chicory
Comfrey or hydroponically sprouted (7-8 days) barley, oats or wheat
Dandelion
Dock
Lantana blossoms
Lettuce
New Zealand Spinach
Shepherd's Purse
Sow Thistle
Spinach
Swiss Chard
Twigs of Willow, Ash, Hawthorn, Acacia, and fruit trees
Watercress

The Philippine Racquet-tailed Parrot and Maroon Mush Parrot are exceptions; they need ¾ ounce (20 g.) chickweed, dandelion or New Zealand spinach; the Kea needs ¾ ounce (20 g.) hydroponically sprouted (7-8 days) barley, oats or wheat, or lettuce.

V. VEGETABLES—per day per parrot

Eclectus Parrot and Senegal Parrot: ¾ ounce (20 g.) cooked sweet potatoes or carrots

Philippine Racquet-tailed Parrot and Maroon Mush Parrot: ¾ ounce (20 g.) boiled sweet potatoes

Amazons, African Greys, Pesquet's Parrots: ½ ounce (15 g.) carrots or sweet potatoes *and* ¾ ounce (20 g.) fresh corn on cob

Keas: ¼ ounce (7 g.) green peas

Lories and Lorikeets: 1/10 ounce (2 g.) grated carrots and 1/10 ounce (2 g.) lettuce

VI. ALL BIRDS: free choice of oyster shell, crumbled, dried chicken egg shell or snail shells, gastropods, quail, mineral blocks, mineral grit, and cuttlefish bone (has to be available at all times).

All large parrots: ½ ounce (15 g.) dog kibble and 1/5 ounce (10 g.) whole wheat bread

All small parrots: ¼ ounce (8 g.) dog kibble and ¼ ounce (8 g.) whole wheat bread

Hawk-headed Parrot and Pesquet's Parrot: 1/5 ounce (5 g.) rice

For all parrots that will accept it: 2-4 mealworms and such

All Lories and Lorikeets: 1/5 ounce (5 g.) evaporated milk

Hanging Parrots, Lories and Lorikeets: 1/5 ounce (4 g.) vitamins

Summing Up

Most imported parrots are taken from the nest while still young, and hand-fed by natives before they are sold. After the quarantine period in our country they are distributed to the pet industry. These primarily-young parrots receive easily digestible food, i.e. boiled and after that chilled rice and corn, a variety of seeds, together with pieces of banana, pear and/or pieces of white bread, soaked in milk, and sprinkled with sugar.

As these birds drink little or nothing at all, medication, such as antibiotics, are mixed with these soft foods. It is advisable to mix vitamins and minerals through these foods as well. A good brand of egg or universal food (available from your pet store) is also a must. Offer these "body building foods" only in the morning, while in the afternoon the new seed-mixture must be provided. The change-over to egg foods and seed-mixtures should be very gradual.

Never make the common mistake of offering a diet consisting only of sunflower seeds, as they do not contain enough lysine (part of the feather pigment and essential to all birds) as well as vitamins and minerals. This is, by the way, the reason why I stress the point of offering egg foods and the like.

Give a good selection of fruits and greens; the majority of these foods contain enough water, while others, like bananas, raisins and currants, have many carobhydrates. It is, however, advisable not to give too much of the latter in order to prevent the breaking up of the nutritional balance. Flower buds, pomes, nuts and small pieces of lean, cooked meat are relished by all Macaws and Cockatoos.

The following seed mixture is, what I could call, a "universal" mixture, suitable for all parrots at all times. It has all the essential amino acids, except lysine. Lysine is found in peas, but as parrot-like birds routinely shun peas, egg or universal foods are used instead to supply birds with enough lysine.

Smaller seeds, such as canary, sorghum, millet, and hemp can best be given in a separate dish, as they will gradually sink to the bottom, and will be covered by the larger seeds and the husks.

The "Universal Mixture"

Barley	5%	Nuts	5%
Buckwheat	10%	Oats	5%
Canary	10%	Rice	10%
Corn	10%	Sorghum	5%
Hemp	5%	Sunflower	20%
Millet	5%	Wheat	10%

Mexican Parrotlet (Forpus cyanopygius)

A Blue-fronted Amazon watches intently as her young hatch from their eggs.
Kers/Beets

4

Breeding Parrots

FOR THE LAST 15 TO 20 YEARS, fanciers have regularly achieved success in breeding parrots, although experience has shown that most psittacines kept as pets seldom multiply. These animals pay more attention to their surroundings and their owners, than to nest boxes and each other.

The choice of a partner is generally difficult as parrots are very fussy, and not every bird of the opposite sex of the same species is accepted.

The animals should be sexually mature and this is usually difficult to determine. If there is no information available on the bird's history, the safest method for breeding is: that all large parrots should be at least five to six years old, and small parrots one to two years old before being considered for breeding.

The true fancier will do his utmost to stimulate his birds to breed, and raise their young. As early as 1888 the first Blue Fronted Amazons were bred in France, while breeding was also successful with the same species in Switzerland, in 1894. Breeding parrots has in fact become common practice now, and our specialized parrot magazines regularly report successful breedings.

The best place to breed a pair of large parrots is in:
1. a spacious aviary (with a minimum length of 12 feet, a depth of 7 feet, and a height of 6 feet with a roost of 6 feet square, and 7 feet high);
2. in a comfortably heated area, as an attic;
3. in a spare room which can be equipped for breeding birds.

An outdoor aviary should have a good night-shelter, and in case of an emergency, must be able to be heated. Thick branches must be provided in the breeding aviary as parrots mate only on them.

Breeding birds must be kept in the best possible condition at all times for the sake of the young one hopes to get from them. These Scarlets are a tribute to the aviculturist who looks after them. They are in superb bloom.   *Kers*

For successful results in breeding Scarlet Macaws, a sufficiently large nest-box is absolutely essential.   *Kers/Beets*

When breedings between psittacine species occur, interesting and beautiful hybrids often result. This eye-catching animal is the result of a union between a Scarlet and a Military Macaw.
Kers

The most suitable breeding period is the spring.

Place various birds of the same species together (if necessary, you can collaborate with a colleague), and observe them unobtrusively from a distance, to determine which birds show interest in each other. The male will court the female by nodding his head, and dance with spread wings and fanned-out tail, offering her food, while uttering loud cries.

When a female is interested, she will show it by accepting the food or a leaf, and by flapping her wings, raising her tail and nodding her head, almost making a bow. This is followed by copulation several times a day. This love-making sometimes continues for over a month, but by that time you will have left the two lovers alone, and have removed the other birds. So do not capture and remove the courting couple.

You should also know about the following phenomena: during copulation and sometimes in between, a foamy liquid will regularly flow from the nostrils of the male. This has nothing to do with a cold however, and is no cause for alarm. The birds will also regurgitate food regularly, which is a sign that more episodes of copulation may be expected. The female will regularly scratch the ground with her feet in one of the corners of the aviary, a phenomenon that we often see with African Grey Parrots. This too is nothing to worry about.

Nest Boxes

As psittacines nest in holes, the aviculturist must provide nest boxes. These can be made of hollowed tree trunks; saw them lengthwise through the middle first, then hollow them out, and glue them together again with cement; or boxes may be constructed of boards with a minimum thickness of 2 inches.

African Grey Parrots and Amazons, birds of about the same size, are provided with nest boxes of a minimum length of 14 inches, a minimum width of 14 inches and a height of 24 inches with an entrance hole of 5 inches in diameter. For Macaws we use a box of 22 inches square, 32 inches high with an entrance hole of 7 inches in diameter. Of a somewhat different size was a box for the Scarlet Macaw that came to breeding in Florida. This box was 24 inches high, and had a surface area of no less than 4 feet by 4 feet. This box was not placed on the ground, but hung on the wall. The nest hollow was covered with a thick layer of sawdust and peat moss. A friend of mine bred a Blue and Gold Macaw successfully in a partially covered orange crate!

Lories are given hollow tree trunks, large blocks of birch wood, or the same nest boxes used for starlings: entrance hole 3 inches in diameter. Cockatoos should be given a spacious box or deep tree trunk which should be 24 inches long and 20 inches wide and 28 inches high; the entrance hole 7 inches in diameter, but usually the birds will enlarge it. Lovebirds and Dwarf Parrots are given boxes or blocks of 6 inches x 6 inches, with a depth of 10 inches, and an entrance hole 2 inches in diameter; the larger species (Lovebirds without the periophthalmic ring) need boxes of 9 to 18 inches in size, with a depth of 9 inches and an entrance hole 3 inches in diameter.

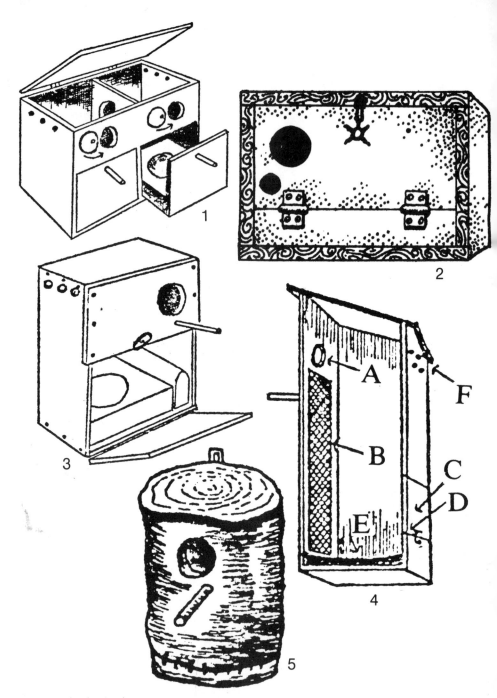

1. A double breeding box of this design is sometimes used for breeding Lovebirds. 2. A front opening nest-box is useful located high in the aviary where a top opening is either not required or practical. 3. A popular, well-designed box providing easy access for the birds and safety both for parents and young. 4. Nest-box cross section: A. Entrance hole. B. Climbing mesh. C. Inspection door. D. Lock. E. Concave base. F. Additional ventilation holes. 5. A Nest-box designed to be closer to natural conditions.

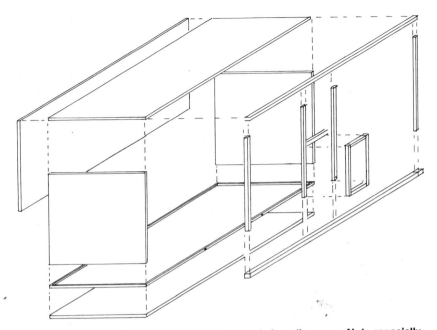

An exploded view of the framework of a well-made breeding cage. Note especially the double floor.

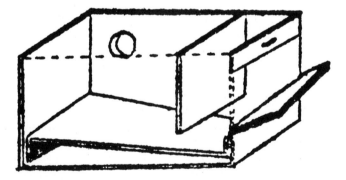

The trap nest-box for smaller species is especially suitable for Dwarf Parrots and Lovebirds that peck at their eggs. Freshly-laid eggs automatically roll down the inclined floor to a partition covered with sawdust or sand to avoid breakage. They are then removed through a small door and placed in the nests of more trustworthy hens.

Incubation Time

The white eggs, of which there are usually two to five, are mainly hatched by the female. The large parrots have an incubation period of about 24-28 days; the smaller birds a few days less. Apart from the Lovebirds, parrots use very little if any nesting material. Yet it is advisable to place a layer of willow branches, dry leaves and moss in the nest box, and to also place some of this material on the bottom of the aviary so that the birds can obtain it, if they desire. Also, don't be surprised if the female gradually removes all the nesting material from the nest.

When birds are hatched, they are blind and have no feathers apart from a little down. The feathers develop very slowly. After 2½ to three months the offsprings leave the nest box, but still need the care of both parents for quite some time, although we can stimulate them to accept food independently. While hatching, the female should be left in peace as much as possible; so do not check the nest box too often.

How to Raise Homebred Parrots

Mr. M. Meiszner, a successful breeder of parrots, especially Amazons, offers his young birds an ordinary parrot seed mixture as rearing food, together with a variety of greens (no lettuce), hard boiled eggs, half ripened corn cobs, plenty of vitamins and minerals, fresh berries, half ripened wheat-ears, and commercial parrot breeding food. A complete composite food for parrots and Cockatoos should contain all the vegetable and animal nutrients, vitamins and minerals a parrot needs every day. Such foods can be moistened with carrot juice and some grated carrots can also be added to the mixture. Every bird should receive a few mealworms daily, as well as a few pieces of chopped raw meat. In the course of several years it has become clear that parrots cannot thrive without animal albumen. Give your parrots a few pieces of horse meat or lamb, veal bones, bones and meat of game regularly. Pieces of boiled egg, curd, young cheese cubes, and butter (also in hard cubes, straight from the refrigerator are also appreciated).

In the aviary of Mr. J. van Dijk (Ijmuiden, Holland) the first young of a male Yellow-fronted Amazon Parrot (*Amazona o. ochrocephala*) and a female Orange Winged Amazon (*Amazona amazonica*) were bred in the spring of 1969; they received daily protein supplement, or another parrot rearing food. When the first young hatched two crushed baby rusks mixed with half a boiled egg, vitamins A and D, were given; one level tablespoon of glucose was also added to the drinking water. During the whole incubation period the adult birds were supplied with pieces of peanut butter sandwich, and a rich assortment of fruits and berries, bananas, and pieces of orange. When the young birds were about 1½ months old, the rearing food was gradually supplemented with boiled corn, and eventually with a normal parrot-seed mixture. Parrot rearing food stayed on the menu. The food was offered to the young birds every 20 minutes, and after some time every hour.

A "Golden Cherry" mutant of the Peach-faced Lovebird scans
its aviary home from atop an excellent nest-box for its species.
Sloots

The nestling in the foreground is a blue mutation of the Masked
Lovebird.   *Sloots*

Normal and mutant Peach-faced Lovebirds.   *Sloots*

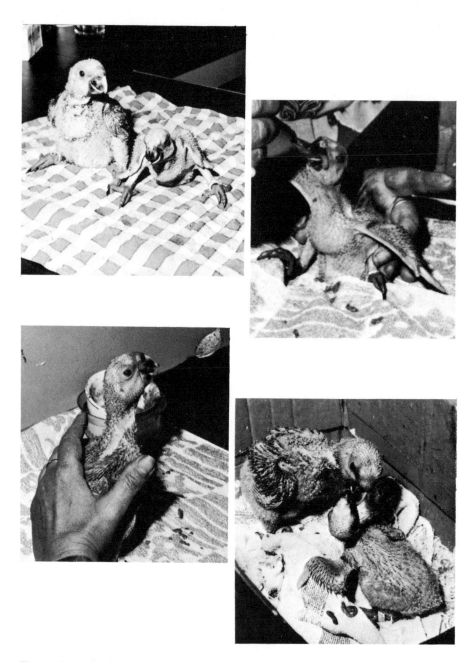

The continental aviculturist Mrs. W. Beets has enjoyed great breeding success with a particular pair of Blue-fronted Amazons since 1975. Every May her birds go to nest and when the baby birds are two weeks old they are taken from the nest and hand-reared by Mrs. Beets. These photos show some of the Blue-front babies and the work that goes into developing them into such personable birds. *Kers*

At first the male gave the food to the female who regurgitated it and in turn offered it to the young.

When all young had hatched both parents started to feed their brood as they would have in Nature!

It may happen, that for some inexplicable reason, certain young birds are suddenly no longer fed. They will screech loudly with hunger, and the breeder must then act quickly. With the van Dijk family one young bird, that was already well-feathered, no longer appeared to be fed, Mr. van Dijk's daughter spoon-fed the unfortunate bird several times a day, until it could take care of itself and eat independently. The animal turned out to be the finest of the three and won various prizes at exhibitions.

In the case of most larger parrots the young are able to leave the nest after two or three months, but they will certainly continue chasing their parents begging for food for six months and more! Only after this period have the bills developed sufficiently for the birds to eat independently.

Young, recently imported birds should be well cared for, which they fully deserve after all the hardships and the long journeys they have experienced.

We offer young, imported birds the following:

Daily—brown bread soaked in water; banana pieces with 3 drops of AD or a multiple vitamin product, plus an orange section with a few drops of these vitamins added as well. Corn boiled daily (which should be boiled less each time) is mixed with soaked and well cooked sunflower seeds, irrespective of kind. Take care to give only well cooked corn immediately after arrival.

A Few Months After Arrival— At this point only well-cooked corn with some partly-cooked sunflower seeds are offered.

Vitamin drops are given on orange sections, but never on whole peeled oranges, as these are not consumed. A few pieces of sweet apple and some bread cubes soaked in milk or water are offered daily.

After Eight Months—Sunflower seeds (uncooked, dry) are added to the menu, also a few unroasted peanuts in the shell, pieces of apple, banana, orange, carrot, fresh branches of willow and fruit trees, corn cobs, millet, spray millet, and vitamins. Do not give lettuce, as it may cause diarrhea. Minerals can also be added to the menu after eight months. A good mineral mix consists of a mixture of digestible calcium and phosphorus to which ground oyster shell, gravel and seaweed have been added. If the minerals are provided daily they promote the development of strong bones and good digestion. Extra additions of oyster, grit, mortar and charcoal are important, as is cuttlebone.

When a bird develops diarrhea—which is likely with recently imported animals—withhold fruit and only offer boiled corn and/or boiled rice. Black coffee along with the regular drinking water is also good. Add some charcoal to the food as well as some millet. Dried seaweed, which contains many vitamins and minerals, including B_{12} which is not found in other plants, can be added to the menu. Adult psittacines may also be given this seaweed.

The Rose-Ringed Parakeet *(Psittacula krameri)* has been known to aviculture since ancient times. A related species, the Alexandrine Parakeet is named for no less a historical figure than Alexander the Great.
Leysen

The Horned Parakeet *(Eunymphicus cornutus uvaeensis),* is an interesting species. It has a crest similar to that of a Cockatiel, but the crest is without erectile power. *Leysen*

The Crimson Rosella *(Platycercus elegans),* a richly-colored species that shares some behavior traits with the Cockatiel. This specimen is a male.
Leysen

5

A Potpourri of
Parrot Pointers

CARING FOR ANY LIVING THING demands a knowledge of what your charges require under all circumstances. This chapter considers those essential items of good parrot management that somehow don't fit into one of the broader categories covered elsewhere in this book.

Acclimatizing Parrots

On the whole, relatively few parrots are offered for sale which have been domestically bred. Nearly all species are directly imported from the tropics, where the climate is much sunnier and warmer than most parts of the United States. Therefore it is quite obvious that all birds will have to adjust to the difference in temperature and light. Although birds are imported throughout the year, there are peaks in export volume. This occurs especially at the end of the breeding season when there are plenty of young birds ready for shipping. This period coincides with the time when it is wet and cold in the eastern United States, so newly arrived birds need proper care and attention.

Whereas psittacines originally arrived in other countries by boat, so that the birds gradually became accustomed to the difference in climate, all modern transport is by air, which means: yesterday they were waiting for transport in a familiar climate, today they are placed in quarantine in a temperature that cannot be compared.

Because of the general condition of the bird it is absolutely necessary that each bird is placed in a separate cage which is spotlessly clean, and that the food be of top quality.

The cage should be cleaned and disinfected every day; if necessary more than once a day. Don't put it off as nothing is more important than absolute cleanliness.

It is advisable to wear gloves (rubber gloves, for example, that can be disinfected) and to wash and disinfect hands and gloves after having cleaned the cage, so that possible diseases are not carried from one cage to the other.

Do not forget to clean food and water utensils very thoroughly every day. Ammonia and a detergent containing chlorine, serve this purpose well. It is best to dilute these with warm water.

Isolation

Newly-imported birds are kept in quarantine in separate cages at a constant day and night temperature of 78° to 80° F.

The number of daylight hours is also of the utmost importance, to guarantee the most efficient intake of food. Personally, I use the following schedule: the light is switched on at five A.M., if necessary, and goes off at 10 P.M. This schedule can be imposed gradually by using a dimmer-switch. Also keep a night light burning so that the birds will be able to find their perches once the main lights have gone out.

Peppermint, the Mouse Repellent

According to Mr. R. Taylor, of Middlesborough, England, mice can be kept out of the aviary by placing small pieces of cloth soaked in peppermint oil, in their holes and passages. It is a method passed down from his grandmother. Mr. Taylor has tried it out, however, and it seems to work! In any case, it is a harmless method, so there is nothing lost in trying!

There are several poisonous products for mice and rats on the market and even products that are harmless to birds. Ask your exterminator for advice.

I personally like Mr. Taylor's method, regardless of the old-fashioned origin, as it is equally safe for man and birds.

Pest Strips

In many breeding aviaries and cages pest strips are being used against mosquitos, flies, and other insects that are too often real "pests" to our birds. Experience of many breeders has taught, however, that use of these strips is ill-advised, as they are harmful to the health of birds. Lovebirds and Dwarf Parrots will not tolerate those strips at all; experience has shown that young birds die within two weeks of strips being installed in their aviaries.

In any pet store you can find harmless insecticides along with sprays against biting lice, feather lice and flying insects, so stay away from pest strips!

The hollow you see high in the trunk of this tree is the nest of a wild Leadbeater's Cockatoo.
Sloots

Here is a Leadbeater's Cockatoo in a comfortable, spacious aviary. These beautiful birds have been known and held in the highest esteem by aviculturists and scientists since the explorations of Captain Cook.
Sloots

Poisonous Plants and Berries

Parrots love berries, fruits, and the like; you should therefore offer willow and fruit twigs daily. In the spring it is usually not too difficult to spoil your birds with blossoms from fruit trees. As long as you know what you are offering, there is no reason not to provide these "goodies."

During the autumn, supply your birds with extra vitamins, besides packaged foods. As a genuine Nature lover, you may often wander about in the woods and fields, enjoying the beautiful scene around you and be tempted to pick wild berries for your parrots.

It is true that wild birds, in general, will instinctively avoid poisonous berries. It is also believed, at least among aviculturists, that red-colored berries are not dangerous at all; for birds that is! Forget it! Wild birds will not eat poisonous berries, but parrots and parakeets are not familiar with most berries, and will eat them as soon as they are offered.

Listed here are the most important poisonous plants, and I would like to add the following thought: whatever is poisonous to man is probably not recommended for parrots and parakeets. Nature is so rich in its variety of berries, that you can certainly leave the following ones alone:

Holly—Serious diarrhea, 20 to 30 berries are fatal for an adult.
Spindle tree—Intestinal upset, fever, palpitations after eight to 10 hours. Two
berries are fatal to a seven-year-old child.

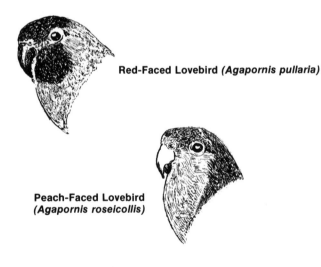

Red-Faced Lovebird *(Agapornis pullaria)*

**Peach-Faced Lovebird
*(Agapornis roseicollis)***

Common Privet—The black berries cause stomach and intestinal upset, general weakness.

Datura—Same symptoms and reactions as common privet.

Lords and Ladies or Cuckoo Pint—The leaves and the berries are poisonous. It only takes a few berries or leaves to give a child fatal stomach and intestinal upsets, hemorrhage, and cramps.

Blue Laburnum—In addition to the seeds and pods of the very poisonous common laburnum, those of the blue laburnum also cause serious stomach and intestinal upsets. From experience, it appears that both the leaves and bark of common laburnum are very poisonous and fatal to birds.

Plants of which practically all parts are poisonous:

Common Rhamnus (Buckthorn)—Commonly found along highways. Very poisonous and also acts as a laxative.

Meadow Saffron—After two to five hours, causes acute stomach and intestinal upsets, burning pain in mouth and throat, shortness of breath, palpitations. After two to three days respiratory paralysis and death.

Lily-of-the-Valley—Poison affecting the heart; irregular pulse, stomach and intestinal upsets, confusion, convulsions, possible death.

Daffodil—Only the bulb is poisonous. Stomach and intestinal infection, fever, headache, confusion, respiratory paralysis.

Snow Drop—Same symptoms as with the daffodil, but here all parts are poisonous.

Spring and Summer Snow Flake—Same as above. All parts are poisonous.

Common Monkshood—Bulb, flower, and leaves are poisonous. Numbness starts in the mouth and spreads to the entire body. Nausea, vomiting, restlessness, chills, severe muscular pains, followed by paralysis and death by respiratory paralysis.

Larkspur—Same symptoms as common monkshood, but less severe.

Purple Foxglove—Poison affects the heart; irregular pulse, stomach and intestinal upsets, confusion, convulsions and possible death.

Live Food

Mealworms should be available to your birds throughout the year, but especially during the breeding period. However, it is certainly not possible for everyone to breed live food. In order to breed mealworms, you must have a few beetles in a crate that measures about 20 x 10 x 10 inches. Drill three holes in each side, each hole having a diameter of about 1 inch. The inside of these holes is screened to prevent escape, and the holes should be drilled at a level of 3/4 inch from the bottom. The crate itself should be lined with plastic or tin to prevent rotting (without covering the ventilation holes that have been drilled in the sides). A properly fitted lid is made for it to halt overly ambitious "travelers" and to lessen the smell a little! The lid should also be fitted with some holes to allow good ventilation, and these can be a little larger than 1 inch in diameter. These holes will also have to be covered on the inside with screen and the rest covered with tin or plastic.

When the crate is ready, fill it with a 2-inch layer of chopped straw. This should then be covered with an old hand towel, on which is placed a layer of bran, about 1½ inches thick. On top of this layer place another old hand towel, on which goes another layer of bran, and so on and so forth, until a level of 1 inch from the top of the crate. All of this is now covered with a cloth, which should not be so thick that the lid does not close properly, and on this cloth you place a small plank of firm fiberboard. It is on this plank that you place the food, consisting of soaked white bread, pieces of fruit, and greens. Once a week we can find the mealworms in the immediate vicinity of the little plank, "ready to serve." All you need do is rinse the worms under the faucet and then give them to your birds.

Keep in mind that some birds should not have too many mealworms, as they are very fattening. A bird so indulged will not be very suitable for breeding any more or perhaps no longer suitable for any purpose. During the time that your birds have young, and also if you have small birds in your aviary, it is advisable to cut the head off the worms, since a live mealworm, swallowed whole, can chew through the wall of the crop, with all of the unpleasant results which follow!

White worms in breeding pairs can be found under rotting wood and piles of leaves. They are small, thin, translucent whitish worms and can be readily bred in a 14 x 14 x 14 inch crate. Fill this crate up with leaf mold and

Panama Amazon Parrots (*Amazona ochrocephala pana-mensis*)

good humus. This should not be too firm, but rather loose, and definitely not dry. Using a trowel, dig a 6-inch hole in the center of the crate. On the bottom of this hole place a slice of soaked white bread and a bunch of worms. The crate should now be closed with a well-fitted plate of glass upon which you place newspapers, making the breeding area dark. Regularly check to see that the soil is not too dry, and that there is still sufficient food for the worms. After a few weeks you can virtually "pick" the worms; just rinse them and your birds will have one of the best foods they could possibly want, particularly during the breeding and chick rearing periods. Good breeding conditions for the worms require a temperature of about 50° F.

Artificial Light

The fluorescent lamps on the market under the brand name "Vita-Lite" (North Bergen, New Jersey) give the bird keeper best results.

The great advantage of these lamps is that they offer the complete scope of natural daylight as well as the beneficial ultra-violet rays. These lamps may seem rather expensive, but as they will burn an average of at least 20,000 user hours the price is comparatively low. This lamp makes it possible to keep parrots anywhere—even a cellar or basement. For a twilight lamp use a normal light bulb of 5 or 10 watts.

Heating

Once the birds have acclimatized, it is important that they are never housed in a cold aviary, even if you have an excellent outdoor aviary with a draft-free and waterproof roost, it remains essential that the birds are housed warmly during the winter months. You can close-off the roost and prevent the birds from flying in the outside flight, or house the birds anywhere you can maintain a temperature of about 68° F.

Home Security

Unfortunately birds are stolen more often than you may think. You can read about it regularly in the papers. Many times it is not even reported to the police, as it is very difficult to retrieve stolen birds.

Since the fancier is left to his own resources as far as the protection of his birds is concerned, it is really essential that something is done, for it is only a matter of paying a handyman for one afternoon. Many exotic bird owners use a highly-efficient, safe alarm system that operates via the electrical front door bell by means of so-called "spring-locks." These brass locks consist of two parts and can be purchased at any hardware store.

Obviously there are quite a few other systems to discourage thieves from taking your birds. Your own circumstances and needs will determine the security measures you take.

African Grey Parrots have been familiar outside their native habitat for centuries. At least one authority believes the species was known to the ancient Hebrews and it is known that King Henry VIII, the Duchess of Lennox and Queen Victoria all enjoyed keeping a specimen. *Kers/Beets*

98

6

Taming and Training

CONTRARY TO WHAT IS SO OFTEN SAID, there is little importance about how a parrot is colored and marked when looking for a parrot to tame and train. Of course, individual differences exist and some birds learn more easily than others, but appearance has nothing to do with this. It is also untrue that only males can learn to talk; I have known hens with vocabularies that many male parrots would envy. If you want to own a talking parrot, look for a young bird, because they are more open to "suggestion," and will want to imitate the trainer without much ceremony. To achieve success, isolate the parrot from his or companions, and even from different species with which he was probably housed in a large aviary. A young parrot, especially a hand-fed individual, makes the best pet. Such birds like to be "cuddled" and handled and will sooner or later imitate many sounds of other birds. Do not give the parrot the opportunity to catch sounds you don't want him to learn, and the bird will give its attention to what you want to teach it. That's what we want to achieve.

Welcome Home

When you decide to purchase a young parrot, two important questions arise, namely:

1. How will you transport a young parrot—which will have to be independent—to its new abode.
2. How will you proceed in order to accustom the bird to its new surroundings?

99

Never collect your new pet from the bird dealer in an ornamental cage. These cages are generally far too big, and even if you were to wrap the cage in newspapers or packing-paper, the bird would flutter about in it wildly, risking injuries. Also, once you get home, you will have an extremely tired and nervous young parrot, of no use for training for some time. So transport your new parrot in a so-called traveling-cage; a "box," usually made of stout cardboard or hardboard, with some ventilation holes or with a piece of mosquito screening. Of course it's possible to make such a cage yourself: the front side consists mainly of small-mesh wire-netting; the rest is made of wood and should measure 20 x 16 x 16 inches. If we use a cardboard box, be careful that the ventilation holes are not covered by labels, wrapping paper or other obstruction. On the bottom throw sufficient seed and also (especially for a long journey) provide some moist bread, so that the parrot will not be thirsty. Don't worry that the bird might not be able to find the seed in the dark; parrots will search for seed in the near darkness of the traveling-cage. During our study-sojourns in Africa, South America, Indonesia and Australia my wife and I regularly saw parrots, parakeets, and other birds as well, foraging during the evening and at night, even if there was little moonlight. Also with the majority of our parrots we were able to establish that the birds searched for food at night. From this we may conclude that transporting parrots over a longer distance is feasible. As long as the birds have been provided with seed (and possibly some moist bread), they can be transported by car, airplane or train in the traveling-cages mentioned above, provided that the time between departure and arrival does not exceed four hours.

On arriving home, make sure all doors, windows and other openings have been closed, that there are no open flames, that the gas or electric stove is not on at the time, and that fans have been turned off. If all that has been done, move the parrot from his traveling-cage to his ornamental cage. The best way to do this is to leave the doors of both cages open opposite each other; usually the bird will calmly climb over, provided it's given enough time.

If possible, make sure the newcomer is settled in its new lodgings before noon, so that it will have all day to adjust to the new cage and the surroundings. It will then also be able to find the various perches with ease and choose one as a permanent sleeping-place. Parrots that are placed in their new abode during the evening will flutter and scramble about restlessly all night. Under these circumstances injuries are likely to happen.

The majority of newly-purchased birds will come from an aviary or a large flight, others will come from the well-known barred parrot-cages, and will therefore be accustomed to seed cups and drinking fountains. Still you must keep a sharp eye on the newcomer—from a distance—and check on whether he has been able to find the seed cup quickly. Most birds learned this at their previous owner's, the birdseller's, or if they were in quarantine, but just to be sure we can scatter some seed on the bottom of the cage. A bird will instinctively search for food on the ground and therefore doesn't have to starve. Even though a full seed cup might be right above its beak, if the parrot is not acquainted with similar utensils, and hand-fed parrots might not be, it might take some time for him to figure out what their purpose is and what's in them. Also the fact that a parrot wants to eat "at ease" after a very tiring journey is easy to understand. If your new bird isn't able to find food immediately, that won't be exactly beneficial to his peace of mind.

Once the parrot has found his food, then this "trailing" the seed in the direct proximity of the seed cup won't be necessary anymore, and you can stop scattering seed on the cage bottom.

First Steps Toward Successful Training

The first few days in a new home are most stressful for a parrot, but you must not give the new bird you wish to train too much rest; start training immediately, and you'll have the best chances for success. As soon as the parrot sits in his ornamental cage, carefully put your hand inside. For these initial overtures a strong, leather glove on your hand could be a wise precaution. The parrot will soon accept your hand as being part of the "furniture" in the cage, especially if you move your hand slowly up and down. More than once, a young parrot has seated itself on my finger or hand within fifteen minutes of its arrival in my home.

Whenever you are occupied with your new parrot, call it by name using a clear voice. Choose a short name like Bobby, Jaco, Polly, Peter or Johnny so the bird will imitate this name without extra "speech-training." If this is not successful you must think of other ways to teach him his name, and I will deal with this fully later on.

As soon as the bird realizes that the hand inside does not change anything in the cage, nor harms him in any way, it won't take long for the bird to accept your hand as a normal part of the cage. One parrot will accept your hand sooner than another; in the latter case you will have to continue your efforts. Don't lose patience under any circumstance, because any unexpected movement of your hand will be experienced as something new. Move your hand slowly and wait until the bird accepts it. That should be your motto!

As soon as the parrot perceives that the hand put inside the cage is not a threat, it will examine it and after it has been approved, your hand will be accepted without much ado, as a "perch."

Once the bird is this far, put an index finger under the body very carefully, and press softly against the abdomen just above the legs; then the bird will usually obligingly seat itself on your outstretched finger. If this does not succeed at first, and the parrot flies away at the first few attempts, continue the first exercise, using the hand as the old familiar seat. If after a few days the hand is once more accepted without fear, try the finger method again.

Obviously, with large psittacines just an outstretched finger is not enough. Two or three fingers works better, or else use an outstretched hand. With small parrots, move the index finger softly but "coercively" across the abdomen; usually the bird will step over onto the finger. If the bird flutters wildly, under no circumstance must you withdraw your hand, as it may

The Red Lory *(Eos bornea)* is a typical representative of the nectar-eating parrots. This beautiful bird breeds readily in captivity and so makes an excellent choice for the aviculturist beginning with *Eos* and related genera. *Vriends*

A not-yet-fully-feathered Red Lory that is being hand-raised. When birds are hand-raised they grow up with no fear of humans and develop into wonderful, gentle pets. *Kers*

assume it has "scared away" your hand, and is therefore likely to repeat the action. Don't withdraw your hand from the cage, before some success, however small it may be, has been achieved.

Outside the Cage

Once the parrot sits on your finger (or hand), without any difficulties, it is wise to teach it also to step back from your finger (hand) to the perch. In order to accomplish this, hold the parrot resting on your finger with his breast against a perch. An order, such as, "up," can be useful. When he fully knows this, it is time to take him out of the cage on your finger or hand. Prior to this several days may have passed. The first trip outside the cage must be of short duration. Of course the parrot will probably at first fly around the room and inspect things. After a few days it will become evident that the bird chooses a special spot, preferably close to mirrors, windows and other shiny objects, wherein he can see himself. Remember these places of preference, so you know where to look for him, if he has left the cage unintentionally. For that matter, letting parrots fly around a room freely is quite risky, considering there may be fragile objects in the room. Also, most parrots have a considerable wingspan and might easily injure themselves in the relatively small space of an average room.

A well-trained parrot will return to the cage immediately if the trainer so wishes; at first lure the bird back with some "goodies;" later on of course these "goodies" will not be needed. Again it is wise to use a fixed command, like "come!" If the bird refuses to "come," despite repeated requests, use a thin bamboo stick about ½" in diameter or a perch shaped like the capital "T" of the same thickness.

The bird will usually climb onto it, especially if you press the stick softly against the abdomen. Slowly, move back to the cage, while the parrot sits on the stick. But it is still important to train the parrot so well, that he returns to his cage immediately after the command "come!" If you have to go "bird-catching" all the time, not only will that be unpleasant and tiresome for the bird, but it will also be frustrating for you.

Once the parrot will return directly to the cage whenever you wish, proceed to the next stage, which is teaching him to go from one hand to the other. Let him jump or step from one hand to the other as much as he wants; this is a very relaxing occupation for you as well as for the bird. When the parrot also understands this, it won't take long before he explores other parts of the human body as well. Finally having reached this point, you really have a hand-tame parrot.

Training With a T-Shaped Perch

A T-shaped perch most resembles a natural resting place and so is an excellent training tool. Many bird-trainers prefer using their finger during the first training sessions as mentioned above, others prefer a T-shaped perch.

Such a perch must never be too smooth, and if it is, it can be roughened up with sandpaper; of course, you should take care that there are no splinters on it.

But before going on, take note of this: perhaps you already know that birds cannot determine by appearance, whether they are dealing with males or females. It's the behavior through which birds recognize gender; for example the generally greater aggressiveness of males when they look at each other. On the other hand, when a hen looks at a male, then the former will slant her head to one side or look away, and more or less ignore the male, or, if she is interested in the male, she will watch him closely while making nodding and bowing movements, her tail spread like a fan, and producing small clattering sounds with her beak. Now you will probably say that this may all be very interesting, but it doesn't have anything to do with the subject, the T-shaped perch!

Well yes, it does! The fact is that it's a serious mistake to point a perch (or finger or hand) straight at a sitting bird and slowly approach it. This resembles an approaching aggressive male parrot.

The only way to approach a parrot with a T-perch is from the side and very, very slowly indeed. As soon as the parrot perceives the perch it is—if you play it right that is—already close to him and he will not want to peck at it, so now you can make the bird sit on the perch by pressing it softly against the abdomen (at the height of the feet). If the bird spots the perch sooner than you mean it to, move the perch slowly away from within its immediate reach and start anew by bringing the perch toward the bird from the side. It is not necessary to start all over from the other corner of the room; you start right where you were standing when the bird perceived the T-perch. If it again backs away from the perch, wait until the bird has calmed down again before making a new attempt. Again you stay right where you were with the last attempt.

The same procedure can be followed to get the bird out of the cage without using the hand-finger method, but with the help of a T-perch. Do not take the T-perch out of the cage until the parrot has learned to accept it as part of the cage furniture. Most cages have a detachable bottom, so the T-perch can be laid on the floor or placed against the bars. Sometimes it appears with this method that the parrot reacts better and easier when approached from behind; the perch is moved across the back and head and under the abdomen in a semi-circle and subsequently the bird is forced onto the perch by light upward pressure. Again, this upward pressure may be strong, so that if there is no reaction the bird is more or less slowly lifted from its seat. If the bird starts nodding nervously and appears to be getting jumpy, it is wise to wait a few minutes until the bird has calmed down again, or else we risk having the parrot fluttering and scrambling about its cage restlessly, which will only make it more upset and perhaps afraid of the T-perch. Obviously, this is far from desirable.

During the whole training-period *talk* to your bird. It doesn't matter what you say, as long as you say something! The human voice often calms the bird and inspires trust in it. And don't give up the lesson unless the bird has made some progress, no matter how small it may be. In the case mentioned above: go on till the parrot has placed itself on the T-perch, and after some well-meant, encouraging words, back to its usual perch. This is accomplished by pressing the T-perch against the abdomen, right next to the feet. This can sometimes be very tiresome for the trainer and it may take some time, but giving up is out of the question; the bird should learn something in a session, even if it is only a little, otherwise the rest of the training will become a difficult and tiresome occupation that you won't enjoy very much, and neither will the parrot!

The Ladder

When after many lessons the parrot steps upon your finger, hand or T-perch without hesitation, you can teach him, now that he is outside the cage, to climb onto the index finger of your other hand or onto a second T-perch. We must not forget to talk to him and praise him if he reacts correctly. Personally I first let the bird step once or twice onto my finger (or hand) or to the second T-perch in this new lesson.

If the parrot has performed it properly once or twice, we put him back into the cage which he considers a "safe harbor."

After having learned something new—however simple that may seem to you—the bird will be enthusiastic, even though it may not be immediately apparent. Therefore, to calm it down, return it to its cage for a little while. After half an hour repeat the process; now let the bird step back and forth four or five times. While perched on your finger or T-perch, it will probably look around the room inquisitively, and even fly around a bit but there is no real harm in that. If the bird is well-trained it will return to your finger, T-perch or its cage when you want it to.

In any case I think it would be sensible not to have anything in the room that can distract its attention (radio playing, phonograph, or TV set). Once the bird is accustomed to stepping from finger or perch back into its cage, the moment has arrived to slowly walk our pupil, perched deftly on either hand, finger or perch, around the room while talking to it. If this has gone well, put the bird back in its cage for half an hour and then try again. A bit of good advice: raise your extended finger, hand or perch a little above your own height if you can; a bird prefers to go to roost as high as possible; it makes it feel safe.

Now you start using the second T-perch, your forefinger or the hand itself. Make the parrot step from one perch to the other or from one forefinger to the other, in the familiar way, by lightly pressing his abdomen; at the same time imitate a staircase by holding the right-hand perch a bit lower than the left-hand perch; the same applies to your fingers or hand. Now make the bird go up or down as you please, as if it were climbing a ladder.

The first time you try this, the young bird will usually start flying about, but if you calmly put it in its cage and try again after half an hour, you'll succeed eventually. Don't make the parrot nervous; if he flutters to the ground, approach him slowly, hold out your forefinger and quietly wait for him to accept it. Follow the same procedure with a T-perch or your hands. Speak to the bird and don't rush things! If he flies or walks away, take your time till he calms down and starts taking in his surroundings inquisitively; then approach him again, while speaking to him calmly and in a quiet voice. Should it unexpectedly be necessary to catch the bird without delay, throw a towel or sweater or something similar over him. Don't try to catch him with bare hands, because a nervous parrot will bite under all circumstances; and bite he can, believe me!

The best way to hold a parrot is to let the bird's back rest against the palm of your hand; the head between your thumb and your middle finger; your forefinger over its head, as if it were a "helmet"; your ring finger on a level with its stomach; your little finger behind its legs or in line with its tail.

Once the bird has learned the "lesson" mentioned above, introducing a ladder will be easy enough. I have found that I obtain the best results when I perform these lessons in front of a large mirror; the bird sees itself, wants to imitate itself and, in short, tries its very best to captivate its reflection; more than once a bird was even so intent on acting up for its double in the mirror that it seriously fell in love with itself. Nothing wrong with that, as long as you give the bird enough attention and leave it alone during its romantic spells.

Ideally, you should start training as soon as possible when the bird is still young, although even older birds can learn a lot if you work intensively with them. Many trainers raise the young birds by hand once they are independent.

When a young, hand-raised parrot doesn't come into close contact with other birds it sees its keeper as its real mother or father, and will irrevocably accept him or her as a member of the same species, however unkind that may sound.

In their behavioral patterns many animals show a tendency to accept the first object they see as a parent and member of the species, especially when there are no other congeners or other animals around. Ducks, hatching from the egg, follow the first object that moves; if that happens to be a human they will follow it. Biology shows many examples of this tendency. Therefore, as you will probably have realized by now, training and taming parrots isn't so difficult as long as you do it with patience and devotion. Because the keeper/aviculturist is seen as a father or a mother and because a bird's behavioral pattern is formed for a large part by copying set examples, certain games are very easy to learn for a young parrot.

Of course, a parrot should never be allowed to spend its whole life in the solitary confinement of a cage without any special attention from its keeper. Petting, conversation and personal interplay greatly enhance the human/bird relationship. Tame, trained parrots may be kept together; if you have untamed birds, keep them away from the trained ones; if you have one trained

The Scarlet Macaw *(Ara macao)* is one of the most beautifully-colored of the genus *Ara.* South American Indians once used this bird's feathers as a form of currency.

The Hyacinth Macaw *(Anodorhynchus hyacinthinus)* looks more like a creation fashioned from velvet than a living animal.
Leysen

The Blue and Gold Macaw *(Ara ara-rauna)*, like the Scarlet is very widely-known throughout the world and makes a very engaging pet.

bird, give it a lot of daily attention—I can't emphasize this enough—but best keep it away from other birds, because it sees its keeper as a friend and a member of the species.

Personally I find it better to keep all trained birds separate. This isn't absolutely necessary however, as I have explained above. Of course you can let trained birds "perform" as a group, but as soon as the performance is over, separate them again; in this way you can prevent the birds from taking over each others' tricks.

From what I have said on the subject so far, it may appear that hand-raised parrots can only be trained with the utmost exertion *if* they can be trained at all. As I have also said, that is definitely not the case. In fact it isn't more difficult to do; it only requires a little more time, trouble and patience. If you are prepared to give your bird the attention it deserves regarding these three points you will certainly be able to turn even somewhat older birds into good performers.

Tricks

You are probably aware that all animals learn through association. The Russian scientist Pavlov demonstrated this with dogs: everytime they were fed, a bell sounded. After some time the dogs would start salivating when the bell was rung, even without their being fed. In other words: Pavlov had taught the dogs to associate the sound of a bell with food. In view of our training, this is an important detail. Reward the bird for everything it does well. Soon it will associate a well-performed trick with a food reward and that the reward is a consequence of its action.

What kind of reward then?

You could try some millet. That's sensible and delicious for any parrot. Birds often get a bit bored when they are in training or during a performance. It may seem as if they can't keep their minds on the subject at hand. The best way to revive their attention is to use a "cricket": the well-known toy that makes a snapping sound when you press the tongue. The birds immediately react to this sound and show a rekindled interest in the game; of course you should reward them for their efforts with a few tasty seeds.

No Food

Before commencing initial training sessions, at least a few hours before starting, remove the food cups from the cage. Once the bird is used to your hand you may hand-feed it. First try some millet or some other seed it likes and snap the cricket as soon as it accepts the food. Every time you give him something especially delicious, make the same snapping sound and before long the bird will associate the sound with the food it likes so well.

What games and tricks can you now teach your bird? There are many possibilities of course and the bird itself will also discover and even design games and tricks on its own. One of my Cockatiels clearly enjoyed taking a coin from my desk and letting it drop into an empty ashtray. Once the penny lay in the ashtray the bird would return for a second coin and repeat this until there were no coins left. Then it would transfer all the coins to the edge of the desk and drop them on the floor. When he had finished this task as well he would fly to the floor, take each coin into his beak and put them in the ashtray once again. If he was willing to repeat the whole procedure more than twice, to the delight of my little daughter, I would provide a food reward in the ashtray and summon him with my cricket to take a well-deserved rest. If he was tired of the game he would come and sit on my shoulder or head, pleased as punch!

Clipping Wings

Clipping a few flight feathers to prevent the bird from escaping before it is completely tame is a side of our hobby on which I don't hold a definite opinion. I have worked with birds that have had their wings clipped as well as with birds that did not and I really couldn't say which birds were the easier to work with.

If you treat the parrot in a calm, controlled manner it will not make a great difference, in my opinion; and of course it may also depend on the spirit of the various birds. I would therefore advise that you start training your birds without clipping their wings. If, however, your pupil proves rather obstinate, clipping a few flight-feathers is a good idea.

If you are for clipping, try doing it on one wing and with a sharp pair of scissors. Clipping a bird's wing won't hurt it, and after a while the clipped feathers will be replaced during molt by new ones. If the bird isn't fully trained when it starts growing new feathers, another clipping will be necessary of course.

Children and Parrots

It's hard to say who gets the most fun out of the companionship: the parrot or the child. From what I said earlier it should be clear that parrots are very affectionate and always willing to play games. Because they are easily tamed and because they can quite literally imitate the human voice, these birds are a constant delight to children as well as adults.

On the practical side, parrots can be an asset to a child's education by teaching children the wonders of Nature. Furthermore, by letting them take care of animals, they develop a love for Nature in general and respect for all living things. Taking care of and caring for birds can give a great deal of spiritual and physical satisfaction.

Talking Parrots

As soon as your parrot is hand tame, start considering speech lessons. If the bird has been raised by hand, directly from the nest, learning certain words and/or short sentences should be fairly easy. You must always realize though that not every bird, raised from the nest, will become an excellent speaker. Teaching parrots, even those a few years old, is possible as long as the trainer works with patience and perseverance. But before starting speech lessons it is important for the bird to feel completely at ease with its keeper.

Also be sure the bird isn't frightened by children nearby, a radio playing or by any other noise whatsoever.

If the bird you're training to talk is frightened during the first few days, only kindness can win back its trust and secure its undivided attention for the things you wish to teach it. This won't happen in just a few days. It can sometimes even mean several weeks of hard work! New birds should therefore always be placed near people so they can observe human activity.

Don't place them too nearby of course, and make sure that household noises or happenings not be allowed to frighten them or make them nervous. Remember that birds that are only given their daily food and drink and which are then left to themselves will never grow tame and will certainly not learn to speak. Constant attention and kindness are needed to make the bird trust and love you and if you can't succeed in this with your parrots, it will be very difficult indeed to tame them and teach them to talk. One could hardly expect any results if that is the case.

Lesser Sulphur-Crested Cock-atoo *(Cacatua sulphurea)*

Galah (*Eolopus roseicapillus*)

Intelligence

It will be obvious to any reader that a bird which talks or performs tricks only imitates; animals can't reason: they cannot "think" in the literal sense of the word; even though the opposite seems to be the case! The parrot is taught to imitate and to repeat, or to do things which have attracted his attention and piqued his curiosity. The bird can only be taught to repeat certain sentences and to use the right answer at the most suitable moments. A bird is not taught to say "Good night" at six o'clock in the morning or to say "Good-bye" when someone pays a visit. The bird is taught to say certain words and/or sentences at the appropriate times of the day.

Male or Female

I firmly believe and I have repeated this often, that the sex of your bird makes no difference to the outcome of its training. Both sexes are equally able to learn to speak and to perform tricks. I have often found that the more responsive birds were the trainer's favorites or special pupils, and nothing more; in no way could he tell the sex of the birds. This is different in the case of the fancier. Then the sex is very important. Only one conclusion is possible here: children and women have the best voices for speech training. The pitch of children's and women's voices makes them easiest for the parrot to imitate.

111

Covering the Cage

There is a tendency to cover the cage of the pupil with a cloth or a newspaper during the first lessons. I don't think that this has a positive result; I have always thought that birds like both to see and to hear the trainer. But this statement is naturally based on personal experiences, and if your bird learns better and faster when it is screened from the world outside, be guided accordingly. Covering the sides and rear of the cage appears to increase the bird's concentration in the majority of cases, because distraction is limited to a minimum.

Demanding Your Bird's Attention

For greatest success, you must fully demand the parrot's attention. Therefore it is absolutely necessary that the bird should not find any excuse not to give this attention. Providing toys, mirrors and such objects is therefore unwise in the beginning: in this way you can't keep the bird fully concentrated on its training in the face of multiple distractions.

It is also inadvisable to train many birds at the same time: two parrots in the same room, even in different cages, is far from sensible, as the birds will imitate each other and do not learn or want to learn what we have in mind.

Abusive Language

Many trainers like to teach their birds all kinds of violent expressions, curses and abusive language. This is very childish and inappropriate. Remember, obscene language may be used by the bird at embarrassing times and in awkward places. I'm not saying that the teaching of curses and such words is difficult; I believe that teaching these words is simplified because of the often sharp and unusual combination of sounds, but this is, in my opinion, a poor excuse for teaching birds things which they do not understand and which might offend many hearers, not to mention the effect on children.

A Sample Training Method

Many a fancier occupied with teaching speech to parrots and parakeets has concluded that the process usually took less time than expected. Children do not learn to speak within a few months. It often takes more than two years before infants formulate anything understandable or sensible. Therefore you must first develop patience if you want to teach parrots to speak; patience and love!

Don't punish the bird if it is not interested, but treat it with love and affection. Experience has taught many trainers that mornings are best for speech lessons, while parrots can also be successfully trained between seven and nine o'clock in the evening.

Blue and Gold Macaw *(Ara ararauna)*

Green-winged Macaw *(Ara chloroptera)*

Blue and Gold Macaw, head study.

113

The cage may, except for the frontside, if desired, be screened and the trainer may place himself where the bird can hear, but not see him, for then the bird's concentration is greater than when it can see the trainer's every movement.

The words or the short expression must be uttered clearly in the same pitch and always at the same speed. Don't say any other expression or other words during the lesson than those which the bird must learn to speak. After every 15 minutes take a five-minute break so the words may sink in.

Make sure that there are no sounds during these breaks: it is sensible for the trainer not to speak with anyone within hearing distance of the parrot and that he not sing or whistle a tune to a song on the radio. After the break, start again with the same expressions, words or whatever you've selected as the subject matter of teaching.

In the evenings go about it in the same way. Don't praise the bird until it has mastered certain words or expressions faultlessly, so that certain sounds and impurities are not taken up with the word that should be learned.

Outside the specific speech lessons, too, it can do no harm to say the word or the expression regularly upon entering the room where the parrot is kept. The morning greeting just as your "Good night" when you turn off the light to go to bed consists of the teaching material.

If, after some time, all your attention and instruction does not work, we will need a different method. Train in a half-darkened room twice a day, for no longer than half an hour per session. Sit with the bird in such a way that it can hear you, but not see you. Sooner or later you will discover that the bird starts repeating the words it has learned. Never lose patience nor punish the bird. Punishing usually has the opposite effect, and the bird will have had enough of speech lessons, not to mention its shattered confidence. We can with a single gesture or word turn a sweet and gentle parrot into a nervous and aggressive creature which is no longer tractable.

Under all circumstances be aware that you are working with animals which ask only your greatest love and which, if it is given to them undividedly, will reward you with strong devotion and affection.

Using Bird Psychology in Training

When teaching a parrot simple phrases like "Good morning" or "Good-bye," practice such expressions when they are most appropriate. The association of time and deed (here: the spoken word) is remarkably strong with parrots and parakeets, mynah birds, crows and related species. Seldom will a bird say an expression out of context if taught properly. When a bird is taught to say the name of a certain seed or a certain type of food, and you practice this when the bird is fed this food, it will soon repeat the name of the food when it sees it. It is also remarkable that parrots find it easy to learn to pronounce the names of the members of the family and to use them properly.

Many fanciers think that training and teaching parrots to speak can be done at the same time. Personally I think it is better first to domesticate them, to tame the animal and then to teach it to speak, but nevertheless many trainers, who give their birds speech lessons and tame them simultaneously, are very successful.

The most common method of taming the bird and teaching it to talk at the same time is as follows: remove food and water containers from the cage as soon as the new bird arrives and hope that the animal has had enough food in transit. I prefer giving the newly-arrived parrot a few hours to get used to cage and food, and then remove food and water trays temporarily.

Early in the morning of the second day the newcomer is fed by hand all the sweet treats he is entitled to. Don't forget to use the expressions or words you intend the parrot to learn. Every time you work with the bird, offer it food. Do this until the parrot faultlessly repeats what you say.

A male Red-Rumped Parrot (Pseph-otus haematonotus).

When the bird is ready for a second expression or a few other words, go about it as above. Eventually, food will no longer be the main stimulus, but the trainer; and the bird will happily learn other words when its trainer is present. By this time you should be able to give the parrot its daily food allotment without additional hand feeding. Your presence, at this point, should be enough for your friend to perform its entire repertoire. Rewarding the bird now and then with a sweet treat is, of course, advisable; your pet store has a whole selection of appropriate treats.

It often happens that a bird stops talking, as soon as you come to its cage. The bird more or less uses what it has learned to lure you to it and once you are there it will look at you with its shrewd eyes and remain silent. If you are about to go away again it will undoubtedly surprise you with a torrent of words and expressions, with the sole purpose of changing your mind and making you stay.

I should point out that it is not wise to stop the lessons after a few words or expressions have been taught, as the first few words are the most difficult to teach. Once the parrot has taken to learning words, then teaching him new words or expressions is, of course, child's play.

You will continually have to give the parrot your full attention, and you will have to continue in the usual concentrated way, and if a review appears necessary, provide one directly. Developing a good talking parrot requires considerable effort.

Tape Recorders

I've heard several phonograph records with detailed instructions on how to train parrots, parakeets and mynah birds, and how to teach them to speak. If you want your bird to learn to speak quickly, a record like that can be very handy, especially if you have Limited time to train the animal yourself.

An excellent record is undoubtedly *Train Your Bird in Stereo* by the famous American aviculturists Henry J. Bates and Robert L. Busenbark. There is also a clear and interesting instruction booklet with the record. To obtain information write the Audubon Publishing Company, 3449 North Western Avenue, Chicago, Ill. 60618.

With a tape recorder at your disposal, you can have enormous success as you can, for example, record the first expression or the first words you would like the bird to repeat. It only requires one extra tape on which you record the lesson needed. Later you can play this tape as often as you like or better still until the parrot can repeat certain words faultlessly. While the bird listens and, hopefully, tries to repeat what he hears, you can leave the parrot on his own and do what you like. A parrot not only imitates the words, but also the intonation and the pitch, and it will therefore be fully concentrating, not realizing whether you are present or not.

Blue-fronted Amazon *(Amazona aestiva)*

Festive Amazon Parrot *(Amazona festiva bodini)*

Cuban Amazon Parrot *(Amazona leucocephala)*

117

After awhile your parrot will no longer limit himself to words or short expressions, but with just as great an effort, will try to imitate the whistling of other birds or the bark of your dog. I have known parrots that could fault-lessly imitate the creaking sound of a wheelbarrow, the squeak of a badly oiled door and grandfather's smoker's cough. A sound can be picked up by the bird as long as the sound which can be imitated catches the bird's attention for long enough and often enough, so take care!

Teaching birds to talk or training them to do all sorts of tricks does not involve any cruelty to the bird, for in the odd 25 years that I have worked with animals, both as a hobby and in my work as a biologist, it has become clear to me that both the bird and the trainer are having a pleasant time together.

Parrots and Technology

Parrots can learn more than 100 words, songs and even sentences which have to be spoken at the right moment. Most parrots will bear with difficulty, however, a radio, T.V. set or phonograph which is playing and they will disregard all words and/or expressions and react most naturally by scream-ing loudly for a long time. They will even compete at screaming the loudest! Parakeets, too, are inclined to do this, and a couple of Budgies or a few Cockatiels in our home will persist in trying to scream louder than my wife's piano playing.

However, most birds seem to be very sensitive to soft, tuneful music for I have often observed parrots, parakeets, Lovebirds or Cockatiels softly swaying their heads to the rhythm of my wife's music.

If parrots continue screaming when a radio or T.V. set is on, then it is best to cover the cage with a thick cloth and the screaming will soon stop.

However, keep in mind that little parrots do not usually pick up a large selection of words and expressions (in comparison with many large parrots, such as African Greys, Cockatoos and Amazons), but they are extremely capable of whistling tunes.

7

Diseases, Accidents, and Parasites

PARROTS PROVIDED with the correct nourishment and housing, free from fumes, vermin and drafts, will rarely become ill. If you take the time and trouble to do things right, your birds should thrive. Quite often the duration of a bird's sickness is relatively short; therefore, if you do not treat the disease quickly it might be too late. For this reason it is important to know their attitude toward other birds and what constitutes their normal behavior.

If you observe, for example, that a bird quite suddenly is sitting in spots in the aviary that it normally avoids, you might take this as an indication that something is wrong. If he is making a bigger mess than usual with his food, this can be a bad sign. If he seems to be sitting in a strange way, again be alert. When a healthy bird is resting he generally sits on just one foot; young parrots are exceptions. If your bird is resting on two (while closing one or both his eyes), then he probably is not feeling 100% healthy.

A bird's plumage should be healthy and smooth, his eyes should be bright, and there should not be any dirt hanging from his feet or beak. Speaking of "smooth" plumage has caused quite a few misunderstandings. When buying a bird, one generally stands very close to the cage; after all, you want to see what you are buying. However, a bird may pass the smooth-plumage test and still not be a healthy bird. Observe the bird you plan to buy from a moderate distance, preferably in his own abode (if possible, not in a transportation or observation cage), and you will soon know if the bird is healthy or not.

Many times small indications imply that a bird is not entirely healthy. Never wait too long before taking action, such as trying to make sure that something is really wrong while waiting for more definite symptoms. It is better to be too early in taking positive action than too late; later if you find your diagnosis was incorrect, after all you lost nothing except perhaps some time. Being too careful is far better than being nonchalant. If you have doubts about a certain bird, carefully catch it and isolate it in a warm, (86°-88° F) (30°-32° C) draft-free area. Since these birds do not like to be confined to small areas, give the convalescent a roomy flight, such as an attic or shed, if at all possible, where you can maintain a constant temperature.

High temperatures make birds thirsty, so they will want to drink more. This affords the ideal opportunity to add soluble antibiotics to their water that will not cause unpleasant side- or after-effects. Always ask your veterinarian about medication. Many such preparations will stimulate the various glands that give resistance to whatever ails the bird. In addition, fertility is promoted and the shine and color of the bird's plumage are improved. In fact, it is a good idea to add a few drops of these antibiotics to the water of your birds every once in a while as a point of routine maintenance.

It is important to check the perches regularly for all kinds of bacteria and insects, since parasites are often the cause of avian illness. Make weekly inspections (every two weeks during the breeding season), being careful not to upset the birds, and you can avoid most serious illness. Cleanliness is absolutely imperative! By paying close attention you can determine whether parasites have gotten into the plumage of your birds. If so the feathers will have a brush-like appearance. Act immediately! Also, if your bird shows signs of losing weight, so that the chestbone sticks out, or if the bird becomes overweight, and has difficulty moving, immediately separate the bird for treatment.

The sick bird's droppings are usually rather watery and of an abnormal color. The last part of the intestine bulges slightly and empties into a cavity known as the *cloaca*. This cloaca is the only body opening for all waste products, sperm and eggs. Since the urine mixes with solid excreta, the feces will never look hard and dry, but on the other hand the feces of a healthy bird are not thin or watery.

The digestive tract of a bird differs greatly from that of mammals. Birds must eat almost constantly. A big parrot can starve if he has to do without food for 35-45 hours or more, and this is just as valid for sick birds. Therefore, never withhold food from sick birds (unfortunately this occurs all too often); try to make the pet eat and preferably its favorite food. Many a sick bird did not die of illness, but of starvation!

Hence you can tell if your parrot is ill by checking the cloacal (vent) opening. This can be checked without catching the bird. If the bottom part of a female bird's body is swollen, she is probably suffering from egg-binding. If the feathers around the vent are soiled, diarrhea or intestinal problem is present, but of course it may be caused by a more serious disease. That is why every aviculturist must read as much literature as possible dealing with parrot diseases.

After a parrot has recovered from any illness, do not, of course, bring it back immediately to its regular quarters. The bird was in a higher temperature as part of its therapy, and to bring it back to an aviary where the temperature is much cooler would be too much of a shock. Your recovered pet would soon be a patient again. Let the temperature in the sick room drop gradually until it reaches the normal temperature of the aviary or room where the parrot's regular cage is located. After that, wait still another few days before letting the bird go back. Choose a sunny day for this, rather than one that is wet and chilly.

Develop your own library on parrot diseases. Although you may be obliged to enlist the help of a veterinarian occasionally, you should be able to act as a very good general practitioner with the help of some of the books on this subject, mentioned in the Bibliography.

Aspergillosis

This disease is caused by breathing in spores, particularly of the fungus *Aspergillus fumigatus.* Certain plants, such as those belonging to the genus

Military Macaw (Ara militaris)

Asperula, can help bring about this fungal infection. Moldy bread, seeds, chaff, musty hay, straw, and similar items can also help cause aspergillosis. The spores produce poisonous toxins that damage various tissues such as in the lungs, nostrils, sinus cavities and air sacs, causing an accumulation of yellow, cheese-like pus that of course interferes with normal breathing. The bird loses all interest in food, with the unfortunate results that it becomes seriously weakened. A bird may even shake its head and stretch out its neck regularly, as if trying to dislodge the blockage. No particularly satisfactory remedy has yet been found for clearing up this problem, and it is best to seek veterinary assistance.

It is very important that the bird keeper always uses fresh seeds, never old or moldy ones. Do not give spilled seed a chance to become moldy; clean the aviary or cage regularly, sweeping up all spilled food. Try to prevent plant spores from blowing into the aviary or cage in spring and fall, particularly if you live anywhere near places where sawdust can be found or where hay is stored. Be particularly careful of wet hay in guarding against spores. Whenever a bird has been infected, the entire aviary or cage should be subject to an intensive inspection followed by a thorough cleaning. Finally, everything must be disinfected. Generally, all the birds will need to be sacrificed. Let us hope that veterinarians will soon come up with a drug that can save affected birds. The aviary or cage can be sprayed with a solution including 1% copper sulphate before any birds are replaced.

Asthma

Fortunately this respiratory problem is rare in parrots, particularly when birds are housed in a good aviary equipped with a draft- and wind-free night shelter. Birds kept indoors suffer from this problem a little more frequently, but asthma is rare enough not to be a concern, providing the care of your birds is sound. The first symptoms of asthma are noisy, difficult breathing and an overall listlessness. If you act immediately there is a chance that a complete recovery can be achieved. There are several good drugs available on the market for the treatment of asthma. Ask your veterinarian for advice; he can prescribe the most recent, and therefore generally the best, drugs available. Place your patient in a bright area where the air is fresh and pure. Give him his usual food, supplemented with fruit, greens, and fresh water.

Be sure you have not mistaken asthma for pneumonia or, more correctly, pneumonitis. With the latter, the lungs are infected and the bird has difficulty in breathing; it makes panting, gasping noises, usually with inhalation but quite often also with exhalation. The droppings are generally green in color, smelly and watery; the bird's plumage is puffed up. Usually a sure sign is that the patient sits with its beak open and also allows its wings to droop. In such a case consult a veterinarian as soon as possible. If for some reason you are unable to do this, place your bird in a warm hospital cage. Cover most of the cage with towels and place a lamp about two feet from the front of the cage to create a constant temperature of about 97° F. (37° C.). Regularly check on the temperature; a second lamp may be necessary if the first one can't achieve the desired temperature by itself. Maintain this temperature for 48 hours or at least until the bird is completely recovered. Use a broad-spectrum antibiotic that has an effect on a wide range of bacteria. According to Arnall and Keymer, tetracyclines are safe and most likely to be effective, but sometimes sulphadimidine may be useful. Ask your veterinarian. As I mentioned before, a parrot will normally drink very little, but the high temperature will change his mind! If he is too sick to drink himself, help him with the use of a dropper. You will need to make fresh formula every day.

Bacteria

The most common form of bacteria causing illness in birds is *Escherichia coli*. If anything is wrong with the bird's food, the bacteria, which live in the intestines, multiply rapidly, often resulting in the death of the parrot. Sulfonamides are known to be a good cure and can be obtained from your veterinarian.

Balance Problems

Both during intensely hot and very cold days, some parrots (especially the smaller ones) have a problem moving and, when they do, have difficulty in maintaining their balance. When on their feet, they fall, and cannot fly straight. A too rapid increase in blood pressure in the various nervous centers, particularly in the brain, brings about these symptoms. Sometimes this is followed by the death of the bird, but in most cases these symptoms disappear spontaneously and quite quickly.

Sulphur-Crested Cockatoo
(Cacatua galerita)

Help matters along by applying a compress drenched in tincture of iodine. In most cases this has a helpful effect. It is also a good idea to place the bird in a separate, preferably small, cage placed in a somewhat dark location.

Blocked or Impacted Crop

A blocked crop will occur at times with young birds, though seldom with older ones, when they have swallowed something. Sometimes this may cause pressure on the windpipe, causing the bird to suffocate. When a situation exists where there is a definite possibility that a bird may choke, it will be quite apparent: the crop will be swollen and breathing difficult. Wrap the patient in a towel and drop a little olive oil in his crop, carefully massaging the mass that is blocking the crop upward toward the beak. Thread and the like can usually be removed by opening the bill as wide as possible and grasping the object with a pair of tweezers. In serious cases the veterinarian will have to perform minor surgery.

Coccidiosis

This is a parasitic disease of the intestine that sets up inflammation; it is fortunately rare among psittacines, especially with birds kept in cages. Birds kept in an aviary may be infected by wild birds that land on or near the aviary, but also when they come in contact with fowl. Usually, however, the disease is brought into the aviary by the infected droppings of sparrows, starlings and other wild birds.

As soon as you notice that a bird has been infected, act immediately. All sick birds must be caught and placed in individual hospital cages and treated with care. Speed is essential because this disease is extremely contagious and can infect the whole population in less than no time. Sick birds quickly lose weight and have a bloody diarrhea. Fortunately sulfa drugs (sulphadimidine, sulphaquinoxaline) and antibiotics will get coccidiosis under control very fast. Here again it is best to consult a veterinarian because playing doctor yourself rarely clears up the problem and usually makes things worse. You'll need to disinfect the aviary; there are several excellent disinfectants to choose from, and no doubt your local pet store will be happy to help you make a choice.

Coccidia are protozoan (one-celled) parasites of different types. The oocytes of cysts of the genus *Eimeria* that come within reach of the birds via the droppings are the cause of the infection. If the cage is not kept immaculately clean and droppings remain within reach of the sick bird, he may re-infect himself and thereby intensify the infection.

Constant Over-Eating

Constant over-eating can occur when birds are given too much sunflower seed or food that is too sweet, to name two causes. Often the germ of over-eating is already planted with the hand feeding of the young birds (giving too many "goodies," for example). Give only good brands of rearing food and the foods mentioned in Chapter 3. Dirty aviaries, vitamin deficiencies and the like can also cause over-eating, which can prove to be a very stubborn condition.

The birds act lethargic. They really look rather ill and spend practically all their time on the feeding dish with their wings hanging down. They look thin and undernourished, and their breast bones stick out. Their droppings are grayish black. The under part of their bodies look rather unhealthy too, sometimes showing a veritable road map of blue and red veins and arteries, in addition to being swollen, hard, and in most cases, infected. In the first place, the menu must be adjusted to the needs of the parrots and the needs of the season. Sweet food must be avoided as much as possible. No egg-foods or self-prepared strength foods should be given for about twenty days. However, you can offer stale white bread soaked in milk or water on a daily basis. Add a little disinfectant to the drinking water. All your bird housing must be sprayed with a disinfectant powder in the evening to rid them of any insects and other small pests.

Constipation

Parrots housed in a too-small area have a greater tendency to become constipated. Insufficient activity, food that is too rich, and eating too much (often done by birds housed in tight quarters) are also causes. If the droppings are expelled with some difficulty and are dry, large, and hard, you can assume the bird is constipated. First consider whether the bird's menu is in order; adding greens and fruit is advisable, as is adding some Epsom or Glauber's salts to the drinking water. It is more effective to put salts into the beak with a medicine dropper. Although these are rather old fashioned treatments, they seem to work very well. A small amount of an oily laxative, obtainable at any good drug store, dissolved in the drinking water or administered with a dropper can bring about a noticeable improvement. Rape seed rubbed in grease can also do wonders. Another good old remedy is to add 10 drops of syrup of buckthorn to the cage's water cup.

A good general rule is that any bird not feeling up to par should be immediately separated from the other birds, and should not be returned until it is completely cured. For safety's sake, where there is some room for doubt, keep the bird in quarantine a little longer.

Common Cold

The common cold is the illness that most frequently affects aviary birds. Most aviaries are not sufficiently protected from wind and drafts, and most fanciers start the breeding season much too early in the year. Temperature differences are another cause of birds catching cold. It is absolutely essential, especially for imported parrots, to get used to our temperatures very gradually. This has made me an advocate of aviaries divided into three

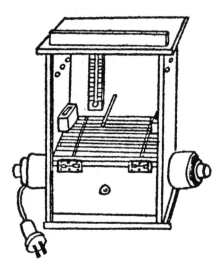

The hospital cage is designed to isolate and monitor sick birds. It provides necessary warmth so important to the recovery of many birds from a variety of illnesses.

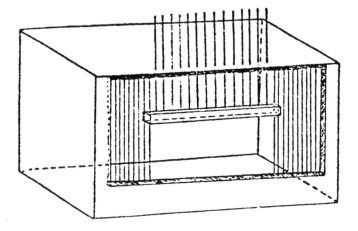

A small traveling cage, such as the one shown above is ideal for transporting parrots and parakeets of appropriate size and for confining a bird temporarily when required.

sections: a closed shelter, a covered flight and a completely open run. Thus the birds can sit and spend the night wherever they prefer; if you condition them gradually by having them stay in the outer aviary whenever weather permits, you will have strong animals that will not catch cold at the slightest breeze.

The moment you first notice that something is wrong with a parrot, isolate him in a warm place. Heat is the first step toward recovery. This is often sufficient therapy, especially if some extra warmth is provided. Obviously, a sick bird should not be placed near or under a window or door that is regularly opened; no draft is allowed, not even during airing.

Special cages heated from below with lamps are available for sick birds, and look rather like small glass show-cages. Opinions vary as to the correct temperature for such cages, but I personally have always had good results with the patients in an atmosphere of around 94.5° F. (35° C.). This temperature must be reached gradually. Never put sick birds immediately next to a heat source. Birds' bones are hollow, and filled with air. Sudden heat makes this air expand inside the bones, not only causing much discomfort and pain, but may even prove fatal.

A patient suffering from a cold is also very well served with an ordinary box-type cage, one side of which receives no heat at all, while the other side is heated with an incubator lamp (infrared radiator—see under DIARRHEA). You can obtain an evenly distributed temperature by putting the lamp at the correct distance from the bars, but try this first with an empty cage. With this arrangement a bird can go to the dark unheated part of the cage whenever it feels it needs less warmth.

Personally I think this is the best method; the bird will not become uneasy during recovery as it might if forced to remain in the heat of the hospital cage. The observant owner will know that a bird is recovering when he sees it spend most of its time in the cooler part of the cage. Of course the heat treatment must initially continue day and night, until the bird's appearance and behavior indicate that it is well again. The smoothness of the feathers is the best indicator of the patient's health.

If a bird suffering from a cold makes sniffling noises and if a slimy fluid issues from its nostrils, while it is also suffering from diarrhea, the cause is probably bacteria (cocci, salmonella, etc.). Immediately consult a vet in such a case. The doctor will probably prescribe antibiotics and advise you to put the bird in a warm place.

Diarrhea

Diarrhea occurs mainly as a result of neglect or malnutrition. At first it can be rather harmless, but when it continues over a longer period it can become quite dangerous, even deadly.

Nervous birds when taken in the hand occasionally excrete thin droppings, but this situation returns to normal as soon as the animals are left to themselves again.

In this connection, it is necessary to carefully monitor aviary co-inhabitants; if big, aggressive parrots are placed in the same aviary with small psittacines, it is easy to imagine that the latter will not exactly lead a quiet life.

Other forms of diarrhea are usually caused by some sort of enteritis. Many causes exist: wrong or contaminated food, a cold caught because the patient was exposed to too many and too sudden changes of temperature, bacteriological infections, etc. Only immediate attention can save them; that is why it is comforting to know that various reliable medications are on the market. In addition to medicines, warmth is very important; maintain a constant temperature of 86°-94° Fahr. (30°-35° C.). My experience is that warmth alone is often sufficient to cure a diarrhea patient.

I have also had extremely good results with an infrared radiation treatment. Irradiate one side of the cage, so the sick bird has the choice of sitting in the radiation or not. In other terms: about half the cage should be out of reach of the radiation. A reliable heating device is recommended because the bird also needs warmth at night. Also keep a small 15 watt bulb burning, so the bird can eat and, above all, drink if it wants to. Give weak black tea or pepperment tea in place of water; I have again obtained very satisfying results with the latter. Mix some pulverized charcoal through the sick bird's favorite food and seed, and administer some tetracycline HC_1, terramycin or aureomycin, as well as preparations which contain vitamins and trace elements. If it appears to be an obstinate diarrhea, consult a veterinarian without further delay. He will have recourse to stronger antibiotics.

Remember that diarrhea is not a disease but a clinical sign, a symptom; it accompanies a great many diseases and therefore should not be treated without first obtaining a correct diagnosis.

Egg Binding

When nesting places, living quarters, diet or other essentials become substandard, eventually some hens will have difficulty laying eggs.

If a hen is too fat, if she is exposed to drafts and cold just prior to laying eggs, if the birds used for breeding are too young, then the direct result will usually be egg binding.

Absence and/or insufficient egg shells can also be caused by a lack of minerals, so that it becomes difficult to lay eggs (wind eggs); in abnormal cases it could even lead to a rupture of the oviduct.

For this reason use only birds in perfect health and of the right breeding age.

The cloaca of young hens is not yet sufficiently developed, and breeding them could lead to complications. Small species should be at least 14-24 months old. Large parrots, like Cockatoos, should have at least passed their fifth birthdays!

Sudden changes in temperature can also provoke egg binding.

Do not let your birds breed too intensively, and under no circumstances permit more than three clutches a year. After the last round, the parents need at least six months rest.

The symptoms of egg binding are easy to discern. The hen has ruffled feathers, usually sits on the ground (often in a corner on the aviary floor), frequently her eyes are partially or completely closed, her vent swollen and red; and often the patient will breathe heavily.

Pick up the bird carefully and place her in a separate cage without perches. Keep a temperature of approximately 94° Fahr. (35° C.). A small quantity of olive oil, introduced in the anus by means of a small brush may bring surprisingly good results. Half a teaspoon of glycerine, dissolved in the drinking water can bring relief. Because of the warmth, the bird will regain command over its muscles and will usually lay its egg within the next few hours. If this does not happen, apply more olive oil to the cloaca. You could also hold the bird over a pan of steaming hot water; but the latter only if the hen has not delivered her egg after one or two efforts.

Where possible, avoid handling the bird to prevent the egg from breaking in the body: often a cause of fatal infection.

A rule of thumb to always keep in mind is to breed only from birds of the right age in an aviary with a constant temperature. Do not forget to mix minerals, vitamins and some drops of cod liver oil through the favorite food before and naturally also during the breeding season. However, be careful with mixing cod-liver oil through the seed: never more than 1½ to two drops per pound.

Egg Pecking

A lack of calcium is often the cause of turning some parrots into egg peckers! In an otherwise smoothly-functioning breeding operation, parrots which start this habit will, of course, need to be "cured."

Boredom can also cause this irritating habit. Apart from cuttlebone and vitamin A and D, also offer them low salt grit and finely ground egg shell. If boredom is the cause, following the same suggestions made under FEATHER PLUCKING.

Eye Diseases

Parrots can easily contract an eye infection when they are exposed to drafts, have insufficient food or have been injured in a fight or mating encounter. Some psittacines are generally susceptible to eye diseases.

We often treat these diseases with eye ointment or eye drops but, unfortunately, without a great deal of success. Actually, I have no objections to remedies, such as aureomycin, and chloramphenicol eye ointment or neocortef eye drops being used. However, sufficient antibiotics should be administered at the same time, either through an injection, for which the vet should be called in, or through crop or beak. In which case tetracycline would be the best choice. Vibramycin, an antibiotic in the past often taken internally by children, may also be used. It has a great number of advantages. Little harm is caused if the quantity given is too great; it may be administered for weeks on end; it can be used as an antibiotic (known as doxycycline) against a wide variety of bacteria, and it needs to be taken only once daily to be effective over a period of 24-36 hours. As to dosage a safe rule of thumb is to administer 1½ to two drops per pound of body weight for about five days.

Eye infections always need to be treated with very great care, as pox, ornithosis, mycoplasm and a lack of vitamin A can also cause blepharitis. The eyes themselves may become infected, as often happens in the case of a cold, and total blindness can follow if action is not taken quickly.

As soon as you realize that a bird is suffering from an eye disease, the only sound advice to follow is: treat it as indicated above, disinfect the bird's cage or aviary and consult a vet. Always be on the safe side. Do not take risks.

Fatty Degeneration

This can occur when birds eat too much, particularly fatty food, and when their housing is rather small as well. The lack of certain vitamins can also be the cause. The symptoms are listlessness and boredom with little or no vocalizing. Sometimes such a bird can even develop bald spots. The birds should first be moved to roomier lodging! This will allow them all the space they need in which to fly and move about. Of course, their menu will also need to undergo some drastic changes. Chapter 3 will provide all the specifics on food for such birds. A lukewarm bath should be provided daily.

Feathers

To maintain the bird's relatively high body temperature of about 106° Fahr. (42° C.), feathers are a vital necessity. To be more precise, the inner covering or down feathers retains the air which has been warmed by body heat. Over these the outer covering feathers achieve more or less the opposite effect—preventing the cold air from reaching the body beneath the feathers.

This is why most surface feathers are usually covered in a thin film of oil, and may also have a thin layer of powder, as in the Cockatoos. This powder or oil film additionally serves to prevent the skin beneath the feathers from becoming wet, leading to a harmful lowering of the body temperature.

You may already know that young birds, whether they are still nestlings or have already left the nest, possess a lower body temperature than adult birds. They need, therefore, some warmth during the night and on cold days, and, if the young birds have left the nest, they should not be unnecessarily exposed to cold, wind, or drafts. This is also why you should never disturb a nest, as this might cause the young birds to prematurely leave the parental home.

There is yet another reason why feathers are important although it is not as evident in the majority of psittacines as it is in certain other genera. Birds often use their feathers as a means of courtship display, so feathers fulfill an important function just before and during the mating and breeding season.

Finally, feathers can be used either as a means of aggression or as a means of intimidation. By fluffing out its feathers a bird can enlarge itself and in this way frighten off a would-be attacker.

The most important function of feathers is, of course, to enable the bird to fly, although there are some species like the ostrich and the various penguins which have lost this ability.

There are three kinds of feathers:
1. contour feathers or pennae;
2. inner down feathers or plumulae;
3. filoplume feathers which grow together in small bundles.

Let us have a quick look at these types of feathers:
1. The contour feathers, as the name implies, give the bird its shape and provide insulation. They cover the bird's body entirely. Each species is usually marked by a somewhat constant number of these pennae at precisely the same places on the body as well as on the wings and tail. The chief feature of these feathers is that they have a rather long shaft;
2. The plumulae provide an extra insulation coat and have little or no shaft. They are found particularly on nestlings and between the contour feathers of adult birds;
3. Filoplume feathers appear to be degenerate feathers which look like hairs. They consist of a thin shaft or several thin shafts ending in a fine plume.

When parrots reveal *bald spots* outside of the molting period, they are caused by parasites. The birds will do a great deal of scratching, too! These parasites, such as bird lice and mites, must be forcefully dealt with. Bird lice usually hide by day in corners and crevices (often in nest boxes and under perches), but come onto the birds at night to suck their blood. Mosquitoes and other damaging insects can cause considerable discomfort to your parrots, particularly during the breeding season. Thanks to various sprays, you should be able to effectively rid your birds of any kind of parasite by using one of the modern, safe sprays for the purpose. Under no circumstances should you use DDT or Lindane, since these are extremely dangerous to birds! Besides, they are currently illegal to use.

Too great a difference in temperature can also cause bald spots on parrots. Quite often we have seen outside aviaries that are partially or even completely enclosed in glass; the temperature can rise so high during the day in such an enclosure that it is more like a hot house than an aviary. The nights, on the other hand, particularly in the spring, are often cold, so the temperature difference is really very great. This can easily cause birds to develop bald spots, particularly on the back and head. Try, therefore, to avoid these drastic differences in temperature. This can be achieved by keeping the aviary open during the day instead of creating a greenhouse, which would be more suitable for tropical plants than parrots.

Baldness, of course, can also be seen during the molting period.

Providing the bald spots do not become too large, they need not concern you. Molting birds need a great variety of food rich in vitamins and calcium. Experience has also proven that it is highly recommended to house your birds in a good-sized flight, allowing them plenty of room for exercise. Exercise during the molt is a very important factor, which should not be neglected. Abundant activity favorably influences the growth of the new feathers.

An annoying habit is *feather plucking;* it can be the result of a vitamin deficiency, listlessness, boredom or overcrowding. It can occur in parrots and parakeets as well as other birds, such as canaries, fowl and ducks. Here again it is very important that their feeding program is carefully inspected and possibly improved. A disinfectant can be added to the drinking water temporarily. Fanciers who do not use city water but instead use well-water are advised to add a reliable disinfectant to the water every day.

Listlessness and boredom can be alleviated by hanging up a few bunches of spray millet or weed seeds. Other suggestions are: sisal rope, which the birds will enjoy climbing very much, and pieces of raw, red meat which will also keep them busy for awhile. Beware of overpopulation. As soon as any birds start this nasty habit of feather picking, they must be immediately put into a roomy cage by themselves.

Once it has become a strong habit, it is difficult to get birds to stop. Only when they have completely given up should they be put back with the other birds. Obviously all feathers should be promptly removed from the aviary or cage, otherwise the birds will start picking at the base of the quill, which contains a vitamin-rich marrow. If this is allowed the birds will never get rid of the habit.

Feeding Instinct

When parrots display their feeding instinct, this is a sure sign of maturity and of the urge to start breeding.

A male will try to win the affections of a female by offering her food, as if to show that not only now, but also later, when she is brooding or has a nest full of young, he is prepared to look after them and feed them. Lonely males of the parrot family by the way, and especially Budgerigars, may be observed smearing reflecting objects in their cages with partly digested food: they have fallen in love with their own images!

Such slimy seed cakes, once regurgitated, are seldom eaten again by the male bird. The owner often thinks something is wrong with the animal, but the phenomenon can be explained quite naturally as stemming from the desire to start a family.

Fractures

Spinal fracture can occur if a bird crashes into a hard surface, like glass, wire, or wood in an unfortunate position. A sudden scare may trigger uncontrolled flight. Avoiding such tragedies is one of many reasons for creating a peaceful environment around your aviary and acting calmly whenever you are around an aviary or cage. There are no objections to small children being allowed to look "at Daddy's birds," and they certainly seem to enjoy this. Do make sure that children behave calmly without too much screaming and arm waving, which is often such a spontaneous and natural reaction for children. With a little insight any mother or father can keep their children under control near the aviary. Obviously, a fractured spine is almost always fatal. More important to us—since we can do something about it—is a fracture of the wing. This is easily recognized, since the bird will sit pitifully in a corner of its cage or aviary, practically incapable of flying. The broken wing hangs almost completely or completely down and cannot be raised to its normal position. Sometimes this misfortune can happen when birds are being caught for one reason or another. Catching birds is a very delicate operation and requires some very careful movements by the captor. The edge of the net must be wrapped with foam rubber or cotton in the event that it comes into contact with a bird you are trying to catch.

It is simple to ascertain the location of the fracture when examining the wing. Using a few drops of an anti-bacterial solution, disinfect the fracture. Many brands have the added advantage of activating the various glands so that the healing process can follow without a hitch. If it appears that only the bone is broken without having injured the muscles and the skin, bring the broken bones together and tape them with plaster. The anti-bacterial solution can always be used even with a normal or spontaneous fracture. After about fifteen days for small parrots, or twenty-five days, for larger species, the wing should have healed. It is advisable, however, to place the bird in a cage by itself in a light, warm location. Feed and water dishes should be placed on the floor of the cage so the patient can easily get to them. There should not be any perches in the cage for obvious reasons. Don't tempt the bird to strain its wing prematurely. Rest is a very important factor in the healing process. Extra vitamin D, calcium, and cod-liver oil are highly recommended and a little fruit now and then, stale white bread soaked in milk, universal food and egg food are also very good.

An exposed, or compound, fracture of the wing, where the bone sticks through the skin, is extremely difficult to treat. Most cases are even impossible for a veterinarian to treat, so it is wisest, unfortunately, to put the patient to sleep. In most cases the exposed end will dry out, die and finally fall off. The bird, of course, can no longer fly. Let the veterinarian decide if anything can be done and be guided accordingly!

A fracture of the leg is also easy to recognize. The bird is on the floor of his cage or aviary and has great difficulty in moving. Quite often the fracture is the result of an unfortunate mishap while catching the bird or the result of nails grown too long.

First disinfect the area of the fracture. Then either wrap a stiff bandage around it or make a splint using a match, little sticks or a chicken quill that has been cut open and affix that to the leg. The split quill must be thicker than the fractured leg—so it is usable only for small parrots. For bigger birds, use ice cream sticks or similar materials. Straighten out the leg by carefully pulling a piece of thread tied to the foot. If the bottom part of the leg has been damaged, it is best to use a quill splint about ½ inch long clasped to the fracture in case of small birds. For the bigger species consult a veterinarian. The splint is fastened with a small amount of plaster or wrapped with cotton or wool yarn. Remember not to tie anything too tightly to avoid cutting off the circulation. A fracture of the thigh is treated the same way for both large and small species.

The patient should be placed in a cage by itself.

The floor of the cage should be covered with a thick layer of sand. Any perches should be removed, of course, and food and water dishes should be readily accessible. Apart from extra vitamin D, calcium, cuttlebone, egg food, and universal food, add a little cod-liver oil to the seed and offer some greens. If the leg does not turn black after a time, then the "operation" has been a success! Should the leg turn blue and later black, this means that the splint was too tight and the leg "died off." It will then need to be amputated. After a month the splint can be removed in the case of small parrots; when dealing with large species, wait 1½ months. Here again, leave the decision to the vet.

To avoid "spontaneous fractures", that is, those without any apparent cause, regularly give your birds vitamin D, as well as cuttlebone, calcium and greens.

Freezing Toes

Freezing toes particularly afflicts small parrots such as Lovebirds, and parakeets; in fact, their toes become frozen at a mere 30° F. (-2° C.), so they must be kept either indoors or in a heated night shelter. Lovebirds are also enthusiastic bathers, even during the winter, so that any bathing water must be removed if freezing temperatures are forecast.

The toes become whitish in color and a little swollen after about a week. At that time the bird will constantly pick at them, because they apparently are very itchy. This nibbling at the toes, of course, leads to bleeding, but strangely enough, the pain seems to stimulate the bird to even more intense picking, with the result that the toes are often gnawed to the bone. You can understand that this causes excruciating pain. Plum-headed Parakeets suffer a lot from this ailment too, but they generally do not attack the toes with their beaks, and after a period of time, the toes rot away.

What, then, can be done? First, move the birds to a frost-free (but not too warm) room. Nevertheless, you must realize that the chances of the toes healing are almost nil. Naturally, this should not stop you from doing all you can to help the birds. Sometimes, particularly if the problem is caught in time, a massage using Vaseline can help to restore the blood circulation and thus regenerate the tissues.

The only advice I can give you is this: if you have birds that are housed in outdoor aviaries, make sure that their aviary has a good night shelter, one that is wind- and draft-free, and in which there are some tight-closing nesting boxes for use as sleeping quarters. In the outer aviary you can also hang a few boxes (without nesting material, of course, to prevent winter breeding). As long as they are draft-free they make ideal winter shelters. Do not give any bathing or drinking water to Lovebirds during the winter; they drink very little by nature anyway, and if they are thirsty they will gnaw at some ice or eat some snow. In the night shelter offer a drinking fountain or automatic water hopper during "long winters," as their shape prevents birds from being able to bathe in them. Also fasten some wire thread criss-crossed over the water's surface so it becomes impossible for birds to bathe in them. This method is highly recommended, because birds may take the opportunity to bathe if given the chance, and their damp feathers will freeze with resulting casualties.

Goiter

Goiter or enlargement of the thyroid gland is particularly common among small parrots and parakeets.

Fortunately, this disorder does not occur very frequently today, because cage sand available from pet shops has often been treated with iodine. It is still widely found, however, in areas where drinking water is deficient in iodine.

Goiter is not usually recognized by an external swelling. The growth, pressing against crop and windpipe, is internal. Clearly, any exertion, such as flying and running, will make the affected bird breathless very quickly. Breathing heavily it will drop to the ground, often with wide-spread wings and pendulous crop and neck. It may also make a high-pitched squeak or wheezing sound with each breath. In order to breathe more easily the bird will often rest its beak against the bars of the cage or on a parallel perch or tree branch. If you do not act immediately, the disease will soon become worse. The bird may start to walk in circles and suffer from infection of the head. Sudden death may then follow due to suffocation, heart failure or weakness due to an insufficient intake of food.

In case of a serious endocrinal disorder the bird may be given iodine-glycerine, i.e. a mixture of one part iodine to four parts glycerine. Alternatively, a mixture consisting of nine parts parrafin oil to one part iodine-glycerine, administered with a nasal dropper in a corner of the beak intermittently over a period of three days, will work wonders.

It is, after all, possible for us, therefore, to play a healing role without too many problems and without having to call in a vet.

Handfeeding the Inappetent Bird

If a (usually young) bird refuses to eat, it must be handfed by teaspoon or feeding syringe.

Boil a quart of milk and dissolve a few spoons of pancake syrup in it while it is still warm. Beat an egg yolk, add a pinch of salt and stir into the milk. If desired 125 milligrams of antibiotics (80 milligrams for small parrots) may be dissolved in the mixture (ask your pharmacist for terramycin or aureomycin). This mixture can be stored in the refrigerator, but should be heated to 80° F. before feeding.

Wrap the bird in a towel, so it cannot bite your hands or perhaps injure or exhaust itself as a result of violent movements.

Place the tip of the dropper or teaspoon in the corner of the beak and give two or three drops of nourishment at a time. Be careful to never really squirt with the dropper. This can easily cause formula to enter the lungs and lead to pneumonia.

Wait after each two or three drops until the bird has swallowed it all. Big parrots, by the way, can take 20 drops per three hours; the smaller ones comparatively less.

If the bird also suffers from diarrhea, give it a few drops of kaopectate or rusk with milk, or follow the instructions indicated under the subject DIARRHEA. Your bird dealer will undoubtedly also have many reliable remedies. Be careful, however, never to administer them simultaneously with the above formula.

Mineral Deficiency

Lack of essential minerals, especially calcium, can result in rickets— particularly in young birds. Those affected will have soft, bent legs on which they can hardly stand. Make sure that they have sufficient intake of vitamin B and D.

Nail Trimming

Birds allowed to climb sufficiently and wear off their nails on rough stones will rarely be bothered with too-long nails getting caught in almost everything. That is why I think flagstones are indispensable in aviaries.

Of course, parrots in cages are much more liable to have trouble with long nails than birds kept in aviaries. Use a sharp, strong pair of nail-scissors to keep nails trimmed, but the job should be done quite carefully to avoid cutting the blood vessels which, by the way, are easily distinguished if the nail is held against the light: the dark lines of the vessels then contrast with the horn. Many parrots, however, have black colored nails; in those cases cut only the tip.

If, however, a blood vessel is accidentally cut, styptic powder can help: press it against the blood vessel with a cotton pad for a few minutes and the problem will be solved. A cotton pad with (non-caustic) iodine will also do.

It is very important to prevent the nails from growing too long. Besides placing a few rough stones on the floor of the aviary, offer perches of several thicknesses, bark-covered breeding boxes and other abrasive surfaces. Small covers are available on the market that can be fitted over perches; these covers are made of sand- or abrasive paper. Also, it can do no harm to provide cage birds with a floor partially covered with sandpaper. Avoid sharp tips and

136

Palm Cockatoo *(Probosciger aterrimus)*

The Lesser Sulphur-crested Cockatoo *(Cacatua sulphurea),* **has been known to aviculture for a very long time. It is a fine pet and worthwhile addition to any collection of birds.** *Vriends*

hooks on the clipped nails which might cause the bird to catch its feet in almost everything.

Obesity

Birds suffering from lack of exercise (because their cage is too small or because their owner has not provided anything to keep them occupied, so that they get bored), as well as those that do not get the right nutrition, are most liable to fall victims to obesity. Getting fat is, however, a very slow process. The owner must watch very carefully to spot the first signs. When the birds can barely sit on their perches anymore, things have already gone too far. The birds sit on the bottom of their cage, panting heavily, and do not seem to want to move. The contours of their bodies have become blurred, heavy and cylindrical and the skin appears yellowish when the feathers are blown apart: the fat shining through the skin! Just blow on the breast or abdominal feathers of such a bird and you will know what I mean.

Parrots suffering from obesity live much shorter lives than those that have plenty of exercise and lively interests. The sick ones have difficulty molting and just sit looking thoroughly bored.

The first thing is to give the birds plenty of exercise: hang some strong sisal ropes in the aviary and a few bunches of spray millet or weed seeds; they will love playing with those.

Then improve their nutrition, strictly by the book if need be, and provide lots of well-washed greens or fruit, free from chemicals, but definitely no food with a high protein or fat content.

With any luck the "obese" bird will soon be his former self again, flying about as sprightly as before. Cage birds must be released every day and allowed to fly freely for at least one to two hours. So treated, every day they will get sufficient exercise and will not suffer from gout. Inside their cages they must also get more exercise. This can be achieved by keeping them in larger cages, or by putting the perches farther apart, so that the bird is forced to make a greater effort to get to the other side. Do not work from the assumption: "my parrot is fat, so if I don't feed it for a few days it will be all right again." The bird must be fed, but with the right kind of feed, for it will perish, however fat it may be, if it receives no nourishment.

Paratyphoid

Paratyphoid is a disease of the intestines, the symptoms of which appear in various forms. The most common form is caused by *Salmonella typhimurinum* bacteria, which are also dangerous to all other mammals, including humans. The illness subsides quickly with young birds, but very slowly with adults. Paratyphoid is often carried by raw eggshells which are fed to birds and is often the result of poor hygiene. However, more often than not, mice and other rodents are the chief culprits for carrying and spreading bacteria. Therefore, be sure that rodents are never able to get into or even near bird houses.

138

Infected birds have no appetite, shiver with cold and sleep a lot. The droppings look white-yellow or green as is the case with diarrhea and the vent is very dirty. Often, in acute cases of the disease, the birds can hardly keep their balance and their eyes discharge a slimy liquid. The birds become inactive and lose weight. If their condition improves you should still keep them isolated. They need to be checked by a qualified veterinarian who will give them antibiotics.

Pneumonia

Pneumonia is usually the result of a severe cold. The patient breathes agitatedly and heavily, and a yellowish slime comes from its nostrils. The veterinarian cannot do anything more than give an injection with antibiotics in the breast muscles, and hope for the best. Keep the bird warm and give it black tea.

Psittacosis and Ornithosis

Also known as "parrot illness," this can be transmitted to humans. Parrots can suffer from psittacosis which is an illness caused by the virus *Muyagawanella psittaci.* Other bird species can suffer from ornithosis which is caused by the virus *ornithosis.* Parrots and parakeets normally import this illness from their life in the wild which is why parrot imports are strictly controlled, with birds kept in quarantine for some time. Affected birds do not want to feed, fluff up their feathers and their droppings are gray-green. If the course of the disease enters its final stage, nervous disorders can be found in those affected. For example, birds can no longer sit on their perches. With antibiotics, it is possible to kill the virus in the early stages and save the birds. But chances of recovery are usually slim with the affected birds dying quickly. Remember that dead birds must be burned.

In *All About the Parrots* (Howell Book House Inc., New York, 1980), author Arthur Freud presents a pertinent overview to the entire question of parrot quarantine as a means of safeguarding public health, native wild birds and the interests of the gigantic American poultry industry. Mr. Freud gives a brief, interesting, accurate documentation of how present quarantine regulations were developed and how parrot species are quarantined under them. He also gives meaningful statistics regarding the percentage of psittacosis actually transmitted by parrot species and the controversy surrounding the use of chlorotetracycline in quarantined psittacines.

As of this writing (1983), there have been no major changes in the quarantine structure or the laws governing it to render Mr. Freud's remarks obsolete. Those wishing to read the entire text of Mr. Freud's discussion are advised to see *All About the Parrots,* pages 27-29.

Tuberculosis

Tuberculosis is caused by bacteria (*Mycobacterium avium*) and infection

139

takes place via the droppings of an infected bird. It can also be caused by bacteria on eggshells or human beings suffering from tuberculosis. To avoid the risk of tuberculosis, the highest level of hygiene is very important. In addition, make sure your birds have plenty of fresh air (without drafts, of course) and sunshine. A bird suffering from tuberculosis loses weight, does not feed and will show blood in its droppings. If an infection is suspected, separate all of your birds from each other immediately. Don't lose any time in disinfecting your cage or aviary with Cresol, 3% Formalin solvent or Chloramin. Any affected bird will eventually die from the infection because, sadly, there is no known cure for tuberculosis in birds.

Make sure your healthy birds are given plenty of vitamins and minerals. Keep them separated for a few weeks until it is clear that the infection has been contained. Often tuberculosis appears as swollen limbs. Many an infected bird will die as a result of a tear in the liver.

Dead birds should be burned and not, as is often the case, stuffed because the danger of contamination remains!

Tumors

Tumors, often caused by infections but more often the result of chemical disturbances, must not be neglected. The clearly visible growths are sometimes only temporary. Many experts on the subject are not yet agreed whether non-infectious growths are caused by chemical disturbances or if we are dealing here with hereditary characteristics.

Symptoms are serious anemia, a definite though gradual loss of weight, nervous disorders, and swelling of kidneys, liver, and spleen. These swellings, as I have had the opportunity to see in a couple of laboratories, can have amazingly large dimensions. Tumors can also form in the ovaries, lungs, intestines, and heart, among other organs. Canaries, parrots and parakeets seem to be particularly susceptible to tumors. Even excessive inbreeding can cause tumors. There is still a lot to be learned about this subject. In the meantime, birds that develop tumors through any of these causes are living on borrowed time.

Worms

The problem of worms in parrots and parakeets is a growing one with which practically every bird keeper is confronted sooner or later. The two culprits are *Ascaridia* and *Capillaria. Ascaridia* are fibre-thin worms, about eight inches long, which live in the upper part of the intestinal tract. *Ascaridia maphrodita,* which are found in the parrot family, are probably prevalent all over the world. They will be mainly found in those birds which forage on the ground, wild birds not excepted. Budgerigars, Cockatiels, Lovebirds, Conures, Asiatic parrots and parakeets and many Australian parrots and parakeets are among the aviary birds found infected with these worms.

Capillaria are extremely thin and transparent, so that it is practically impossible to detect them with the naked eye in the bowel contents. These tiny worms also live in the intestines, surrounded by the catarrhal slime engendered by their irritating effect on the intestinal wall. With a little of this slime prepared on a glass plate we can observe the *Capillaria* worms under the microscope. They have the approximate thickness and length of a mouse hair.

Both *Ascaridia* and *Capillaria* are true parasites: only the eggs can survive outside the host body. Worms driven out with an anti-worm treatment die quickly and are no longer infectious.

Parasitic worms have developed into extremely efficient egg-production machines. Tests show that an *Ascaridia* worm can lay between 2000 and 3000 eggs a day, in other words: one million eggs a year. Since an infected bird usually carries several worms, it will be obvious that there may be millions of eggs on an aviary floor. *Capillaria* do not produce so many eggs.

The worms' eggs leave the bird together with the droppings. Newly excreted eggs must ripen first; they are not infectious for a number of days.

The most dangerous period is during humid, warm weather, when the process takes about ten days. During the cold months it runs very slowly or stops altogether. Nevertheless the eggs retain their developing power.

As soon as it gets warmer the eggs will ripen. Most are ingested by the birds together with pieces of soil, hardly ever with food. Once inside the body the eggs will develop and the worm will attach itself to the inner wall of the bird's intestines. The larva will live for about a week, after which it dies and becomes part of the bowel contents. The *Capillaria* will remain more or less in the same spot; the larva is fully grown after approximately six weeks, when it can lay eggs in turn.

The environment will be infected when an infected bird deposits its droppings. In certain weather conditions the eggs may be carried through the air to other places, so that the contagion spreads.

Luckily, worms' eggs are rather frail, but they are very resistant to cold and moisture. Dry weather and intense sunlight kills them off. Eggs exposed to direct sunlight will die in a few days, but only in hot and dry weather. In other conditions they can survive all hardships, even for a year or more!

Worms' eggs are very light and small, they may end up anywhere. They may float from one aviary to another and when a person steps in infected soil he is liable to infect any other aviary he enters.

Worms often cause the death of the bird they inhabit, through hemorrhagic enteritis, when they pierce the intestinal wall. In any case, an infected bird is always weakened.

Since the worms are constantly surrounded by partly digested food, they can consume the best of the proteins, vitamins and minerals. The intestines start expanding due to the multiplication of the worms. A cluster of worms finally blocks the passage and in the final phase the bird dies from shock.

To ascertain the cause of a bird's death, have an autopsy performed, since *Ascaridia* are easily discernible. *Capillaria* can only be seen under the microscope. The bird must be opened so that the intestines come out, after which the droppings can be pressed from the intestines with a knife, spatula, or other flat object.

If the infection is serious, the swelling of the intestine indicates that it is filled with worms, that have blocked the intestinal canal completely.

Usually, the many worms are not very big. However, sometimes real "giants" may be found among them and when observing these specimens, even a layman won't question the menace of these pests.

How can you prevent this infection?

Every bird has a certain resistance against parasites. If this were not so, all our aviary birds would be doomed to die. However, when a bird is in poor condition, or has a shortage of certain nutritious elements, his resistance is lessened.

It has been proven that aviary birds and poultry, nourished with albumin-rich food and vitamins A and B, are better protected against worms and the harm they can do to the body, than birds not so provided for. Parrot-like birds need regular supplies of clean grit. Do not simply scatter it on the aviary floor, but provide it in trays, so that there is little danger of the birds picking up worm eggs from the ground.

The covering of the aviary floor is also an important consideration. If the aviary floor is earth or sand covered, when moistened by rain, it will be an ideal incubator for worm eggs. Therefore, a gravel or concrete floor is recommended, as worm eggs soon dry out and die on them.

Never place newly-purchased birds in with the other animals in the aviary before making sure that they are wormed. It is therefore wise, when exchanging or buying birds, to convince yourself that they are duly wormed. In this respect, mutual trust between fanciers is vital.

Nevertheless, if you want to be absolutely sure, place the newly-purchased bird in an indoor cage. If it proves to be in good condition, after a few days worm it. To be one hundred percent sure, repeat ten days later.

This method, especially placing the newcomer in a separate cage, is not possible for everyone, of course. While it is not absolutely necessary to follow this procedure, the certainty that the birds will be worm-free without it will be lessened.

How to treat the worm-infested bird?

About 15 years ago, a small tube containing a capsule, was used. This tube with a rather sharp upper-side, was forced into the beak. With much patience (if, in the meantime the bird had not become so frightened that shock was close), one could attempt to push the tube about an inch into the beak. Following that the capsule arrived in the bird's crop through a small hose positioned in the tube. If one was lucky the capsule would enter the crop, if not it could just as easily get into the trachea, which could be fatal. If, in that event, the bird wasn't given a strong shake, head down so that the capsule could be expelled from the trachea, the animal would die.

Fortunately times have changed and there are various reliable and effective products obtainable that are less dangerous or unmanageable.

Worms, found in parrot-like birds, will not appear in other birds.

I personally have my doubts about the above pronouncement—avoid all risks and use the best vermicide for parrots and parakeets. These include L. Ripercol®, L. Narpenol®, and for the European market, Ovorotol®.

How do we proceed when worming?

Many modern fanciers know that worming via the syringe or crop-needle is the most common method used. To those who are not familiar with this, it will seem difficult to put the crop-needle into the crop of the bird. Some aviculturists who have bred parrot-like birds for many years, still do not dare use this method and will ask a friend or fellow breeder in their bird society to do it for them.

If you don't like handling the crop-needle, then there is still another effective method to vermifuge, by using concentrates. I have personally used this method over the last years successfully, along with the crop-needle.

If your birds are accustomed to concentrated food, it is easy to mix the vermicide with these goodies; the birds will certainly ingest it. Just take the normal portion of concentrate the bird eats within 24 hours and add 1/3 cc Narpenol to it; regardless of the size of the bird being treated.

Tests have proven that an eventual overdose scarcely bothers the bird and should this be so, then only during the first 48 hours.

If you have birds, however, that refuse concentrates, you will be compelled to use the syringe.

Mixing the vermicide with the food has the advantage that the bird absorbs it all. Alternately, when using the crop-needle, some birds vomit the whole lot. In that case it is advisable to keep the bird quietly in the hand so that it won't vomit, waiting till the fluid has mixed with the contents of the crop.

Goffin's Cockatoo *(Cacatua goffini)*, **an interesting species, long-established in aviculture.** *Ebben*

Many fanciers mix the vermicide with the drinking water, but that is the last method I would recommend. This method never gives any certainty. A sick parrot barely drinks (unless he has warm lodging) and, as you know, parrot-like birds are seldom found near the drinking fountains.

Whatever vermicide you use, repeat the treatment after ten days. This is the time the worm eggs at the bottom of the aviary take to ripen and a second phase takes place in the bird's body. After this second cure the worm cycle has ended, as the worms are not full-grown and therefore cannot produce eggs.

This only applies if the aviary floor is thoroughly refreshed by digging up the ground deeply to at least 17-20 inches.

You can also scorch the ground with a blow-torch, a method I personally prefer. Afterwards I still dig up the ground to a depth of at least 17 inches. Other disinfectants won't be sufficiently thorough and I only trust the method described above.

Observe your birds regularly and when one of them is not well-feathered outside the molting period, don't wait until it is too late, but take precautions and measures immediately. There is a good chance that a worm infection is involved and that the bird can be saved.

Other good advice: if you have a sick bird, place it in a warm hospital cage so that it can recover a little and endure the worm treatment better.

A final remark: in case of a severe infection with a bird in great distress, it is advisable to reduce the dosage of vermicide to a quarter of the normal dose. A large dose kills all the worms at the same time, and may cause constipation of the intestinal canal. Twenty-four hours after this treatment you can give the bird a normal dose, if necessary. After the treatment keep it in the cage for several days and give it the best delicacies you can find, including vitamins and unripe grass and weed seeds.

Worming several times won't harm the bird; this has been proven scientifically, and those fanciers who think that by excessive worming the animals become sterile are wrong. Worming doesn't reduce the fertility of the birds at all.

External Parasites

Birds infested with mites or lice are rather restless, and their movements and posture betray their discomfort. Their general state of good health deteriorates. Chlorosis, anemia, gluttony, inflammations, bare spots, and a great many infectious diseases can follow as a result of insects and parasite bites. The female that is sitting on eggs or has young in the nest may desert them. Young birds still in the nest that are attacked at night by red mites (*Dermanyssus avium*) usually die. The most common parasites are red mites (a real source of trouble), feather mites and quill mites (*Mallophaga*), mange mites (*Cnemidocoptes*) and mosquitoes. Several of these species will come at night in great numbers, sit on the birds and suck blood; others, like feather and quill mites are constantly present on birds. The "night-visitors" hide during the day in various recesses of cages and aviaries.

144

The only way to exterminate these pests and avoid recurring visits is a regular and careful control of cleanliness. Inspect the nest boxes at night. If you see any insects, use a small amount of a safe commercial spray, following the instructions on the label. Effective acaricides are malathion and gamma benzene hexachloride for red mites and iodine, antihistamines and sulphur ointment for feather mites. Also dust the parrot with insecticide power. In severe cases one can even see the nits of eggs on the small feathers and the shafts of the birds. Good results are given by a dichlorvos strip; such a strip works for about four months. Be careful that neither the bird nor its food come in contact with the strip!

Mange mites cause leg calcification; the chalky nodules are easily removed by repeated rubbing with vaseline, olive or salad oil.

Warmth

Although most psittacines can endure temperatures down to 48° Fahr. (8° C.) quite easily, the majority prefer a little more warmth: about 61°-76° Fahr. (16°-25° C.). From this data you can determine when to move the birds to their night shelter or, failing that, to an indoor location away from frost. If necessary lightly heat the night quarters with an infrared radiator. Frost is always dangerous; birds that spend the night outside in the run may get frozen toes (see FREEZING TOES), especially those that rest so high on their legs that the toes are not protected by a warm "blanket" of abdominal feathers. Of course you must harden all birds gradually by forcing them to often roost outside in spring and summer whenever weather permits. Once the birds are accustomed to temperate climate and to their accommodation they will be extremely hardy and seldom fall ill. Only when sudden temperature changes are expected, and every bird lover keeps an eye on the weather forecast, must you take precautionary measures to protect birds from heavy rainstorms, sudden frost, strong winds and other extremes of weather.

Preventive Hygiene

I consider it most important that every bird lover who handles sick birds, see himself as a potential infectious disease-carrier. Therefore it is absolutely necessary to wash one's hands thoroughly after touching and handling a sick bird, before going to a second bird. Rubber gloves must be disinfected and sterilized by boiling after treating a sick bird.

I have noticed that washing the hands is rarely mentioned in the literature of bird fanciers, but they should know better!

Finally, one more piece of advice at the end of this, in some respects, less than cheerful chapter. It is clear that I couldn't possibly cover all the health problems and illnesses related to psittacines in this chapter; the space being too restricted. Therefore, every bird lover should acquire a good book on bird diseases to serve as his own pharmacy. The bibliography of this book mentions a number of helpful titles.

Citron-crested Cockatoo (*Cacatua sulphurea citrinocristata*).

8

A Guide to Parrot Species

ONLY A TRULY ENORMOUS, SCHOLARLY BOOK can deal in detail with all the known parrot species. Therefore a selection has been made with emphasis on the better-known parrots. In the event an aviculturist has a bird that is not mentioned in the text, he is advised to read the notes concerning *Family* and/or *Genus* for the nearest related species. If one follows these notes, he will be well advised regarding care, housing and proper feeding.

Family: *Cacatuidae* (Cockatoos)
Subfamily: *Cacatuinae*
Genus: *Cacatua* (White and Black-billed Cockatoos)

The impressive Cockatoos are predominantly white or salmon pink in color. Their habitat is from the Philippines up to and including Australia. They are stout animals with a white and black, very strong beak or bill, with a striking big yellow or pink crest that can be spread like a fan, especially when afraid or excited, or during courtship. In the open country Cockatoos are extremely lively birds that are constantly on the move. Their acrobatic stunts will fascinate aviculturists, provided the birds are housed in a large aviary. Even as a colony together in the field, along the edge of the woods, in parks and gardens, they attract much attention. In the wild, Cockatoos usually try to avoid human settlements and remain extremely vigilant and alert at all times. As soon as they scent danger they fly away. Together the birds go to the feeding grounds and drinking places in the morning and late in the afternoon, and together still later in the day they fly back to their sleeping place. Each bird goes back to the same tree in which he has his own branch!

Cockatoos feed on all kinds of fruits, nuts, berries, seeds, mushrooms, roots, bulbs, twigs, leaves, blossom, buds, melons, ripening wheat and rice crops and probably insects and their larvae.

They nest in tree cavities, in rotted sections of a branch, in caves and other hiding places. The female produces two to five white eggs that in turn will be incubated by both sexes, although the hen is more active than the male.

The majority of imported Cockatoos are hand-tame, and often familiar with the food supplied in captivity. This is understandable as the natives capture the young from the nest and raise them by hand, often with those foods as well as with boiled rice and/or corn on the cob. The Sulphur-crested Cockatoo and Salmon-crested Cockatoo are especially well-known for their friendliness and ability to talk, so they are frequently captured, and imported to the United States and Europe.

Through his highly active nature the Cockatoo is capable of quickly learning all sorts of tricks in no time at all, but as a talker he is definitely no genius, especially compared to Amazon Parrots or African Greys. It is also a pity that quite a few Cockatoos never lose their habit of screeching, often for attention; Cockatoos are sometimes real screamers! However, I have known Cockatoos that were very quiet indeed, and the reason is simple: in their native country they were raised with love, care and understanding.

Cockatoos are easily tamed and therefore worth your full attention. In captivity, supply the well-known commercial parrot seed mixtures, as well as cooked corn on the cob, wheat, oats, canary or white seeds, spray millet and other millets, fruits, nuts, lettuce, dandelion and chickweed among other foods. Watch out though, as the birds often tend to eat only what they like, and not what they actually need. Variety in the menu is the most important factor in the life of any cage or aviary bird.

Through the years it has become apparent that males (who, by the way, usually have black-colored eyes) are much easier to tame than the females (of which the majority have brown-colored eyes).

A pair kept in a large aviary usually become attached and quite often will attempt to breed. It is evident that the aviary should be built with very strong materials, as one constructed from timber will change, due to the birds gnawing nature, into a wreck in no time at all.

During breeding time a pair of Cockatoos is far from tame, however; they only have eyes for each other, and no longer for the aviculturist. Birds in the mating season preen their feathers constantly.

It is interesting to note, that the word "Cacatua" is of Malayan origin; it means "old father" ("old" in the sense of "wise"—"kaka" = father; "tua" = old).

Furthermore it is known that Cockatoos can grow to be very old; birds of 60-80 years and more, are quite common. They often remain with the same family for many generations.

148

It runs in the family. On a visit to the world-famous Walsrode Bird Park (Germany), young Tanya Vriends, the author's daughter, inspects a Cockatoo's nest. *Vriends*

Leadbeater's Cockatoo *(Cacatua leadbeateri)* is a familiar species often found in the company of Galahs. A raucous, destructive bird, Leadbeater's does well in an aviary, but is not generally recommended as a cage bird. *Vriends*

In order to satisfy their gnawing desire, Cockatoos must have willow and fruit tree branches daily.

Leadbeater's Cockatoo *Cacatua leadbeateri* (Vigors)

DESCRIPTION: Striking salmon-pink and red colored crest, with white tips. In the center of the red section, a yellow band (females have a broader band than males). Head and breast are salmon-pink, darker near the wings. The rest of the body is predominantly white. Bill is white, with deep dark brown iris in males, light reddish brown iris in females. Legs and feet of both sexes are gray. The immature birds resemble their parents at a very early stage, although they still possess pale brown irises. Only after approximately three years do the eyes of young females turn to a light reddish brown.

LENGTH: 13½ inches (34 cm)

DISTRIBUTION: The dry woodlands of Australia, except in the farthest southwest. The birds can be found on grassland, near small tree-groups and in scrubland, in parks and gardens, especially close to water. They remain on the ground the greatest part of the day, looking for food. In some regions the population is becoming rather small, although in other parts of the country they seem to increase in numbers, especially where enough fresh water is available.

These shy birds often live together with Galahs. The trees in which the birds sleep are easily recognizable, as the branches haven't any bark left. Early in the day, and later in the evening, when the sun goes down, they fly to several drinking places; sometimes hundreds of birds are gathered together—it is quite an unforgettable sight! They feed on different kinds of *Acacia* and other similar seeds; as well as on fruits, nuts, roots and berries; in New South Wales even on paddy melons, *Cucumis myriocarpus,* and wild bitter melons, *Citrullus lanatus* (Forshaw).

There are two subspecies:
1. *C. l. leadbeateri,* and
2. *C. l. mollis,* from Western Australia.

SPECIAL NOTES: This highly-priced aviary bird is only suitable for a large aviary. As a cage bird I don't think he will be appreciated, as he is usually far from friendly and likes to scream loudly and irritatingly. The aviary must be built of strong materials, as he is very destructive.

The Leadbeater's Cockatoo, Pink Cockatoo or Desert Cockatoo has hybridized with the White Cockatoo, the Sulphur-Crested Cockatoo and the Galah. This is, in itself, especially interesting, as he is usually very spiteful in mixed collections, even when kept with more than one pair in the same aviary.

The bird may breed in captivity, especially when offered hollowed-out trunks. In the nest-hollow, deposit some peat-moss, and every two days one egg is laid. During the day the female broods, in the late evening and at night the male incubates. After 21-22 days the chicks hatch and are taken care of by both parents. Extra sunflower seeds, peas, wheat, oats, chickweed, dandelion and white bread in milk are necessary during breeding and rearing time. Soaked seeds, germinated seeds, commercial parrot rearing food and corn on the cob are also a must. Some zoos recommend a couple of mealworms per day per bird during the mating, brooding and rearing period.

Good results can be expected when the birds have a partly decayed tree trunk, with an opening about 34 inches deep, with a diameter of 10 inches. The bottom must be covered with peat moss. Don't expect results too quickly.

A breeder from California had a pair since 1903, and they started rearing their first family in 1940. So, if you don't possess patience, you had better look for another hobby!

Lesser Sulphur-Crested Cockatoo *Cacatua sulphurea* (Gmelin)

DESCRIPTION: General plumage immaculate white, with yellow wash under the wings and on the abdomen. Clearly visible yellow ear-coverts. Iris, feet and legs gray-black. The female has a red-brownish iris. Immature birds possess a light colored beak, also their feet and legs are lighter than those of the parents. After two years the beak colors to its definite tint; after those two years the young are fully colored and appear indistinguishable from their parents.

LENGTH: 14 inches (34 cm)

DISTRIBUTION: Widespread in Indonesia; probably introduced to Singapore, and quite abundant. Lives in open woodlands, along the edges of forests and in cultivated fields. They are extremely fond of coconuts, but eat all kinds of seeds, fruits, nuts, berries, grubs, roots and even insects.

There are six subspecies:
1. *C. s. sulphurea,* from Celebes, Buton Island and Singapore (introduced?);
2. *C. s. djampeana,* from Alor, Djampea, Kaju adi, Kalao, Kalao tua, Pantar and the Tukangbesi Islands. This subspecies is smaller than the nominate species;
3. *C. s. abbotti,* from Solombo Besar, with a pale yellow cheek patch;
4. *C. s. occidentalis,* from Flores, Lombok, Noesa Penida and Sumbawa, with very little or no yellow in the feathers;
5. *C. s. parvula,* from Samao and Timor, with a smaller beak than the nominate form;
6. *C. s. citrinocristata,* from Sumba, with orange, instead of yellow ear-coverts and crest.

SPECIAL NOTES: In captivity the birds breed regularly, especially when the pair has been together for a few years. During the mating season the male circles around his chosen bride, nodding his head regularly, and even taking small hopping steps, now and then. If after a while the birds start to preen each others' feathers, things are going just right! The female lays two to three white

Lesser Sulphur-crested Cockatoo *(Cacatua sulphurea)*.   *Ebben*

153

eggs that are incubated for 25 days by both sexes: the male during the day, the female during the night (the reverse of most Cockatoo species). After approximately 60 days, the chicks leave the nest, but will still be fed by their parents, for quite some time. While being fed, the young birds will flap their wings. Two weeks after leaving the nest they can forage independently from the ground.

The birds are regularly obtainable from pet shops, and it is not too difficult to form a true pair. In a large aviary these birds are really impressive. As cage birds I don't think them too suitable, as their ability to speak is quite limited. They are, however, far from noisy!

Mr. Kates feels that they are not as intelligent as their Australian counterparts, and, therefore, do not respond well to trick-training. Experience has taught us that young, domestically-raised Cockatoos become extremely affectionate and trustworthy.

Greater Sulphur-Crested Cockatoo *Cacatua galerita* (Latham)

DESCRIPTION: Predominantly white, with some yellow on the base of the cheek and throat feathers, and ear-coverts; the underside of the tail and flight feathers have a yellow tinge as well. White periophthalmic eye ring, without feathers. Beak, legs and feet are dark gray. The iris of the male is deep brown; the iris of the female brown-red. Immature birds resemble their parents, but with gray-brown color patches on the crown and on the back of the wings. They still possess brown irises.

LENGTH: 19.5 inches (50 cm)

DISTRIBUTION: North and east Australia, New Guinea, Melanesia, and introduced to New Zealand.

There are four subspecies:
1. *C. g. galerita,* from eastern and southeastern Australia; this is the largest member;
2. *C. g. fitzroyi,* from northeastern Australia. The bird is smaller than the nominate form, has a pale blue periophthalmic ring, and not as much yellow on ear-coverts, cheek and throat;
3. *C. g. triton,* from West Irian, Papuan Island, New Guinea, and surrounding islands, and introduced to, among other areas, Indonesia. This subspecies has the broadest crest;
4. *C. g. eleonora,* from the Aru Islands, and similar to *C. g. triton.* I hesitate to accept this subspecies, as Forshaw does, as a valid subspecies.

There is only one living specimen available of unknown origin.

SPECIAL NOTES: I think that this species is the most talented Cockatoo, but it takes quite some work and patience to tame them. They rarely breed. The female lays two to five white eggs, which are incubated by both sexes; during the night the female broods, during the day the male. When approximately 2½ months old the young leave the nest. Nestbox: 35 x 22 inches.

154

The Umbrella Cockatoo *(Cacatua alba)* is also known as the Great White Cockatoo. *Vriends*

Sulphur-crested Cockatoo *(Cacatua galerita),* a large species famed for its size and overall grandeur.

The Umbrella Cockatoo *(Cacatua alba)* makes a striking picture when its crest is raised.

155

Moluccan Cockatoo *(Cacatua moluccensis),* **also called the Salmon-Crested Cockatoo, is a beautiful and personable bird.** *Ebben*

Moluccan Cockatoo *Cacatua moluccensis* (Gmelin)

DESCRIPTION: The Moluccan Cockatoo is indeed a majestic bird. The body is white with a salmon-pink wash, and the broad, elegant crest is also salmon-pink. There are also some small feathers in the forehead, which are white, with salmon-pink shading also. The inside tail feathers are cream, the white periophthalmic eye ring has a faint bluish tint. Beak, feet and legs are gray-black. The female's head is a little smaller, and the salmon-pink colors are not as intense and do not occur as frequently as in the male. The iris is dark brown. After one to two years the pink colors will appear in the young.

LENGTH: 19.5 inches (50 cm)

DISTRIBUTION: The southern Moluccas.

SPECIAL NOTES: These birds grow tame and affectionate in no time at all, especially towards children. As soon as something occurs which they don't like, they start screeching. On the other hand they are good whistlers, but far from excellent talkers. This species has been bred quite regularly. The two to five white eggs are incubated for approximately 25 days. The pair of Mr. K. Oehler (Germany) raised young with success in 1974, 1975 and 1976, although breeding this species remains difficult. The birds require a large, strong aviary.

Umbrella Cockatoo *Cacatua alba* (P.L.S. Müller)

DESCRIPTION: This is a predominantly white bird (except for some yellow on the inside of wings and tail). The broad crest looks like an inverted umbrella, hence the name. The periophthalmic ring is pale blue. The beak, legs and feet are gray-black. The iris of the male is brown. The iris of the female is red-brown. Immature birds cannot be distinguished from their parents, except for their gray eyes and dark, almost black, feet and legs.

LENGTH: 16 to 18 inches (40 to 45 cm)

DISTRIBUTION: North and south Moluccas. The birds usually live in pairs or small groups. They love to stay high up in the trees, looking for food. They frequent coastal areas and forests. Their food consists of all kinds of nuts, seeds, fruits, berries and insects.

SPECIAL NOTES: They breed regularly; the birds require a large aviary, and nestboxes of 19½ x 16 x 19½ inches. After 2½ months the young leave the nestbox. Don't disturb the birds during the breeding season, as they are extremely nervous and alert at this time.

The Umbrella Cockatoo is no great talker, but exceptionally gentle and very easy to tame.

Blue-Eyed Cockatoo *Cacatua ophthalmica* (Sclater)

DESCRIPTION: This bird is irregularly found in captivity. It takes its name from

Red-vented Cockatoo *(Cacatua haematuropygia)*, from the Philippines.
Ebben

Ducorps' Cockatoo *(Cacatua du-
corpsii)*   *Ebben*

158

the blue periophthalmic ring. The bird is predominantly white, with a black beak and dark gray legs and feet. The crest is yellow. The male has a dark-brown iris, the female a red-brown one. Immature birds are barely distinguishable from their parents; they have a grayish-brown iris and darker feet and legs.

LENGTH: 19.5 inches (50 cm)

DISTRIBUTION: New Britain and New Ireland in the Bismarck Archipelago. The birds live primarily in the rain forests and in the mountains, up to 3000 feet. For most of the year they remain in groups of approximately 10-20 birds, they are very common, and forage for nuts, berries, all kinds of seeds, insects and grubs.

SPECIAL NOTES: Not commonly imported. The birds seldom breed in captivity. The female lays two eggs; the incubation period is approximately 30 days; both sexes hatch the eggs. A friend of mine had a breeding pair of which the young stayed in the nestbox for four months.

These Cockatoos are not great talkers; they are rather quiet and non-aggressive.

Red-Vented Cockatoo *Cacatua haematuropygia* (P.L.S. Müller)

DESCRIPTION: Predominantly white birds with occasional yellow and salmon-pink colors around the ears, and near the base of the small, broad crest. Quite some yellow on the inside of the wings and (especially) on the tail. The vent is reddish to orange. The periophthalmic ring is white-blue, the beak whitish gray; feet and legs gray. The iris of the male is brown, the female's reddish-brown. Immature birds are similar to their parents.

LENGTH: 12.5 inches (32 cm)

DISTRIBUTION: Philippines and Palawan. The birds live in and near woods and cultivated agricultural land and such. They are handy, quick fliers. They particularly love to eat corn and different seeds, fruits, berries, and roots; as they are primarily corn-eaters, farmers often shoot them in great numbers.

SPECIAL NOTES: These freely-imported birds are the smallest of all Cockatoos, make very nice pets, are good talkers and quickly learn all sorts of tricks. As breeders, however, they do not possess such fine qualities, at least not in captivity. The San Diego Zoo (1979) reared three young from one pair.

A Red-Vented Cockatoo hybridized with a Leadbeater's Cockatoo female in Bush Gardens, Tampa, Florida (1973). The young were predominantly white with some salmon-pink on wings and crests.

Bare-Eyed Cockatoo *Cacatua sanguinea* (Gould)

DESCRIPTION: Predominantly white birds with a recumbent crest and a blue-colored periophthalmic ring, which has a large swollen area just below the eye.

159

Head, neck, face, cheeks and crown feathers are white with a salmon-pink base. Flight and undertail feathers are yellowish. The beak is white, feet and legs gray. The iris is dark brown. Immature birds do not possess such a large eye-ring, and I refer particularly to the swollen area below the eye.

DISTRIBUTION: Most of Australia except for the coastal areas, and reaching into New Guinea. They frequent mainly open plains, preferably near water. They seldom stay for long, but prefer to wander about. They live in large groups, and are extremely noisy. Their diet includes nuts, berries, seeds, fruits, insects, grubs, greens and roots. As they also consume a large amount of rice, the farmers would rather see them go than come!

SPECIAL NOTES: The Bare-Eyed Cockatoo, also known as the Little Corella, is fairly rare in captivity, although they are probably the best talkers among the Cockatoos! They also like to play games and perform tricks, but they are noisy and will destroy a wooden cage or aviary in no time at all. The first breeding success occurred in the London Zoo (1901), but Mr. F. E. Blaauw achieved success in Holland (1926) too, as he managed to breed his pair for many years in succession. Exceptionally productive was the pair from the San Diego Zoo, that reared no less than 103 young between the years 1929-1970. Apart from the age of the birds (look at the last date, please!) which in itself is astonishing, the caretakers raised the young by hand-feeding. Mr. Bertagnolio (Italy; well-known for his success in breeding the Lesser Sulphur-Crested Cockatoo), in 1975 raised one young, the next year two. The sad part of this story is that the male bird killed his mate in 1977, during incubation; the young birds were saved, and hand-reared.

In many zoos and bird parks breeding successes are recorded quite regularly. In general the female lays three to four white eggs; after the young have hatched they open their eyes at about eight to ten days; after nine weeks they leave the nest.

By observing eight pairs in the wild it became evident, that they usually have three broods per season; it is also very possible that the birds mate for life. On more than one occasion the Little Corella hybridized with other Cockatoos; the most interesting one being the mating with a Galah in the Wroclaw's Zoo in Poland.

Long-Billed Corella *Cacatua tenuirostris* (Kuhl)

DESCRIPTION: Predominantly white; orange-red forehead and band across the throat. Head and upper breast have orange-based feathers. The underside of the tail as well as the flight feathers are deep yellow. The beak is white; the upper mandible is long and curved. Feet and legs are blackish-gray; the iris dark brown. Immature birds are not to be distinguished from their parents once they have left the nest. Only the blue periophthalmic ring, with a large area of bare skin just below the eye, is smaller and their irises are still grayish-brown.

160

LENGTH: 15 inches (38 cm)

DISTRIBUTION: Southeast and southwest Australia. There are two subspecies:
1. *C. t. tenuirostris,* from the southeastern parts of Australia and
2. *C. t. pastinator,* from the southwestern areas of Australia. This subspecies lacks the orange-red band across the throat, and the orange colors on head and upper breast are also missing; the rest of the body is white. Both species can be found in savannahs, forests, woodlands, grasslands and grain fields. These Cockatoos are noisy and rare. Thanks to the long upper mandible they are able to dig for roots, bulbs, and so forth; they also eat berries, fruits, nuts, grubs, insects and larvae.

SPECIAL NOTES: These delightful pets are known to be very intelligent, and talkative, although they will start screeching as soon as something displeases them! They also kick up a racket if left alone for too long. They demand regular attention.

In the wild they breed high in gum trees. They also breed regularly in captivity. In the San Diego Zoo pairs are fed snails and mealworms, which apparently, stimulates their willingness to breed. In 1959 the first time a pair bred they were in a large aviary with a nest which was 4½ feet deep and which was placed on the ground. Only the female incubated the eggs; after 29 days the chicks hatched and both parents took very good care of their offspring. They were fed on sunflower seeds, corn on the cob, wheat, peas, slices of apple, carrots, sweet potatoes, bread, vegetables, fir seeds and peanuts. It is advisable to cover the inside nestbox with a layer of wood chips.

Genus: *Eolopus* (Galahs)

Although *Eolopus* shares certain anatomical similarities with the Genus *Cacatua,* there are also some important differences. Mr. Holyoak (1970) examined the cranial osteology and pointed out structural peculiarities (Forshaw). Galahs possess a short crest, are of medium size and predominantly pink and gray in color. The bare periophthalmic ring is prominent and sexual dimorphism is only very slight. They prefer to live in open country, and forage seeds, buds, roots, bulbs, grubs, insects, berries and fruits. Studies show that, as Galahs live in large groups, they are extremely harmful to wheat crops; calculations estimate that 5000 birds eat approximately 30 tons of wheat per year! This is why farmers destroy their nesting places in trees, forcing the birds to seek the coastal areas. To date we even find Galahs in Tasmania.

Galah *Eolopus roseicapillus* (Vieillot)

DESCRIPTION: White forehead, crown and ears, with shades of salmon-pink. Rest of the body pink also, except for the gray secondary wing coverts and wings. The beak is light horn-colored; legs and feet are gray-black. The iris is

161

A pair of Galahs. This species is sometimes also known as the Rose-breasted Cockatoo.
Vriends

The four Galah nests in this one tree give some idea of how prolific the species is and why it occurs in such large numbers through almost all of Australia.
Sloots

162

dark brown in the male, pink-red in the female. Immature birds are much drabber looking, while their breast and head are not yet shaded with gray. Their irises are still brown.

LENGTH: 14 inches (36 cm); the female is somewhat smaller.

DISTRIBUTION: Australia and Tasmania. They prefer to live on cultivated farmland, eating grain crops. They are far from shy, and breed even in parks and large gardens. They travel in great flocks, often with other Cockatoos. There are three subspecies:
1. *E. r. roseicapillus,* from eastern, central and northern Australia;
2. *E. r. assimilis,* with darker shades and more pink in the crest; the periophthalmic ring is lighter. This subspecies is from western Australia;
3. *E. r. kuhli,* similar to the *E. r. assimilis,* but with a grayish-red color in the periophthalmic ring. As stated before, Galahs wander about with other Cockatoos, especially with Sulphur-crested Cockatoos. I have heard them flying at night. They search for food on the ground, but enjoy sitting high up in the trees, from where they fly back and forth to and from the ground. They feed on roots, seeds, green shoots, buds, wheat, oats, rice, insects and larvae.

SPECIAL NOTES: Before copulating, the birds play about, nodding their heads, with raised crests. The male makes some soft-sounding noises, while running with small, quick steps over a thick branch towards his bride-to-be. As soon as he has approached her, she runs off, hiding herself between the branches and leaves; but he follows her swiftly. The female lays two to five white eggs, which are incubated by both sexes for approximately 30 days; in captivity sometimes in twenty-one to twenty-four days. After hatching the young remain in the nest for 1½ months; after fledging they receive the care of both parents for another month. In order to get proper breeding results, moisten the nestbox regularly. Use boxes of 22 x 20 x 40 inches or 55 x 50 x 100 cm (40 inches or 100 cm is the height), while Mr. W. de Grahl recommends boxes of 14 x 14 x 22 inches or 35 x 35 x 55 cm, with a nest entrance of about 3½ inches or 9 cm in diameter. When large boxes are used, fasten a strip of mesh on the inside in order to make it possible for the birds to leave their "maternity room" easily.

Kates states correctly that Galahs "have a tendency to become overweight, and that they often develop fatty tumors, usually near the vent. These tumors are usually benign and can be removed quite successfully." Therefore it is absolutely necessary to feed your birds with lots of greens, buds, berries, dandelion roots, and kale. Don't offer too many sunflower seeds; in general, cut down substantially on foods that are high in protein. The birds also enjoy a daily supply of fresh twigs.

Galahs are playful, friendly and fairly good talkers, in short one of the most pleasant Cockatoos one can imagine.

The Gang-Gang Cockatoo *(Callocephalon fimbriatum),* like the Eclectus Parrot, exhibits sexual dimorphism to a marked degree. In this species the male has a larger, more elaborate crest than the female and his head plumage is a vivid red. Harder to find than the white Cockatoos, the Gang-Gang is nevertheless an attractive pet and a worthwhile addition to any avian collection.   *Vriends*

Genus: *Callocephalon*

A remarkable, identifying feature of these birds is the large crest, the tip of which curves toward the beak. The broad lower mandible enables them to split hard seeds, such as Eucalyptus seeds. The sexes are easily distinguishable.

Gang-Gang Cockatoo *Callocephalon fimbriatum* (Grant)

DESCRIPTION: The male is dark gray; the feathers of head, wings, shoulders and abdomen have white bases; those bases are yellow or orange in the female. In addition the male has a red head and partially red cheeks. The female possesses a smaller crest, grayish in color (as is the rest of her body). In both sexes the beak is light horn-colored; the iris of the male is dark brown; while that of the female is gray. Immature birds initially resemble the female, but the red colors soon appear in the young males. The beaks of the young remain dark brown for quite some time.

LENGTH: 13 inches (34 cm)

DISTRIBUTION: From southeastern Australia to deep in the southern parts of this "parrot country." They are also to be found in Tasmania and on King Island; the birds were most likely introduced to Kangaroo Island, which is under Adelaide, South Australia.

The birds inhabit mountain forests, wooded valleys, parks and large gardens. During the breeding season they live in pairs or small groups. They forage in trees and shrubs and seldom come to the ground except mainly to drink or to pick food, dropped from a tree. Next to Eucalyptus seeds, they feed on nuts, berries, fruits, insects and larvae.

SPECIAL NOTES: In the wild, Gang-Gang Cockatoos breed high in a tree cavity, near water. In captivity they need a large aviary and a big nestbox 20 x 20 x 24 inches (50 x 50 x 60 cm); the entrance hole must have a diameter of approximately 3½ inches (9 cm), but the birds will, while breeding, constantly gnaw on this entrance, and so demolish in one season practically the whole front of the box. The splinters the birds obtain from their gnawing activities are used for the nest. The two eggs are incubated by both sexes for approximately 30 days. After two months the young leave the box, but will be fed, for at least a month or more. After three or four years the young are no longer distinguishable from their parents.

These highly intelligent and comical birds are not suited for life in a cage.

They are rare on the pet market, and extremely expensive. Many an aviculturist endeavors to locate a pair, as they have fine personalities and are good talkers. In Europe, unlike the United States, they are quite common and frequently bred.

Genus: *Calyptorhynchus* (Black Cockatoos)

These large, black-colored Cockatoos, have short crests, and colored tail bands. The tail itself is very long and round at the end. The large beaks of the different species are "clearly adaptations related to feeding habits" (Forshaw).

165

The Yellow-Tailed Cockatoo *(Calyptorhynchus f. funereus)*, a spectacular member of the intriguing family of black Cockatoos. *Leysen*

Black Cockatoo *Calyptorhynchus funereus* (Shaw)

DESCRIPTION: A predominantly blackish-brown bird, with yellow feather margins. The underparts are duller and brownish. The beak is dark-gray; the iris brown. The periophthalmic ring is reddish, legs and feet brown-gray. The female has brighter yellow cheek-patches. In the yellow tail band there are more small black spots in the female's than in the male's. The beak is horn-colored, and the periophthalmic ring is dark gray. Immature birds look like the female, but the eye-ring is duller in coloration.

LENGTH: 26 inches (67 cm)

DISTRIBUTION: Southeastern and southwestern Australia, and on Kangaroo Island and Eyre Peninsula. They inhabit wet coastal forests, deserts, orchards, mountain woodlands, pine plantations and occasionally the drier inland areas as well. In large flocks they even visit the wheat-belt in southeastern Australia, the mallee and arid scrublands.

There are three subspecies:
1. *C. f. funereus,* from the above-named areas; this bird is often called Yellow-tailed Cockatoo, for obvious reasons;
2. *C. f. baudinii,* from southwestern Australia, south of the Murchison river; this subspecies is known as White-tailed Cockatoo;
3. *C. f. latirostris,* from the dry areas of southwestern Australia; this subspecies is similar to *baudinii,* but smaller in size.

SPECIAL NOTES: The Black Cockatoos are rare in captivity. The birds are shy, not only in the wild, but in captivity as well. They usually function in pairs or flocks, and are notably garrulous. As soon as there is some danger they attempt to hide high up in the Eucalyptus trees. They eat berries, fruits, seeds, buds and many insects and their larvae.

There are some other species of Black Cockatoos, although they are very rare and seldom offered for sale. The Red-tailed Cockatoo (*C. magnificus*), from eastern, northern and western Australia (with four subspecies), and the Glossy Cockatoo (*C. lathami*), from eastern Australia are two examples. They require the same care as the Black Cockatoo despite their rarity.

It is, finally, interesting to note, that during an autopsy Sir Edward Hallstrom discovered that the species of this Genus do not possess a gizzard, but a kind of a second crop, next to the "regular one." This organism resembles a small sack and is probably used to store food temporarily.

Genus: *Probosciger* (Palm Cockatoos)

There is only one species known. The bird is black, with a large beak, naked cheek-patches, a prominent crest and a black-tipped, red tongue. It is noteworthy that the remarkable red cheek-patches change to a bright color when the bird is excited; my daughter Tanya says that "this is the only bird in the world that can really blush like I do!" The cere is covered with small black feathers, but the thighs are bare.

Palm Cockatoo *Probosciger aterrimus* (Gmelin)

DESCRIPTION: Black, with red cheek patches. The bill is grayish black, feet and legs are gray. The iris is dark brown.

LENGTH: 24 inches (60 cm)

DISTRIBUTION: Most of New Guinea, and the adjacent islands of Misool and Aru. They are also known in Australia on the Cape York Peninsula (northern parts of Queensland). The Palm Cockatoo is the largest Australian psittacine.

They spend the greatest part of the day high up in the trees of jungles and rain forests, but they also live on savannah land and in scrubs. They enjoy digging up roots, bulbs, seeds (especially the seeds of *Pandamus* palms) and grubs, but also forage berries, fruits, leaves, buds, insects, and their larvae.

There are three subspecies:

1. *P. a. aterrimus,* from Misool and Aru, and Northern Australia;
2. *P. a. goliath,* from the Papuan Islands and West Irian to southeastern Papua; this subspecies is indeed the largest, the "Goliath" among the Palm Cockatoos;
3. *P. a. stenolopus,* from New Guinea and West Irian; the crest feathers are narrower than those of the *goliath*.

SPECIAL NOTES: In captivity these gentle, but rare birds breed regularly. Mr. R. T. Lynn of Sydney, Australia, received a pair in 1968 that were thought to

Palm Cockatoo *(Probosciger aterrimus),* a bizarre-looking, yet gentle bird. *Leysen/Vriends*

Amazon parrots form one of the largest of psittacine families including some of the rarest and most familiar hookbills. Shown here are Finsch's Amazon *(Amazona finschi)* at left and the Orange-winged Amazon *(Amazona amazonica)*. Both display the typical stocky body and green plumage common to most of these delightful birds. *Leysen*

The Cuban Amazon *(Amazona leucocephala)* is considered an endangered species with a ban on importing. An excellent talker, it was the first New World parrot species brought back to Europe by early explorers. *Leysen*

169

The Yellow-winged Amazon *(Amazona aestiva xanthopteryx)* is a subspecies of the familiar Blue-fronted Amazon. It differs from the nominate form in showing a yellow, rather than a red bend at the wing. This species is also sometimes known as the Bahia Blue-fronted Amazon. *Leysen*

The Blue-headed Parrot (*Pionus menstruus*) is a typical member of the genus *Pionus*. These birds bear strong structural similarities to the Amazons, but are noticeably smaller than most Amazons and have red undertail coverts as compared to the green of the Amazons. *Leysen/Vriends*

170

The Red-throated Amazon or Jamaican Parrot (*Amazona collaria*) is a rare species seldom seen in captivity although several hundred passed through U.S. quarantine stations in 1979.   *Leysen*

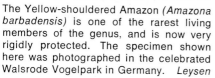

The Yellow-shouldered Amazon *(Amazona barbadensis)* is one of the rarest living members of the genus, and is now very rigidly protected. The specimen shown here was photographed in the celebrated Walsrode Vogelpark in Germany. *Leysen*

The Blue-fronted Amazon *(Amazona aestiva aestiva)* is one of the most popular of all parrots. The species is considered a good talker and breeds readily under favorable aviary conditions. *Leysen*

The Spectacled Amazon *(Amazona a. albifrons)*, the smallest of the true Amazons, is widely distributed among bird fanciers all around the world. The species is known by several familiar names including White-fronted Amazon and White-browed Amazon. They breed readily and make good pets, but tend to be rather noisy.

The Red-lored Amazon *(Amazona autumnalis)* is yet another Amazon species with a variety of names. This bird combines all the most attractive features of the genus and will also breed when provided with favorable conditions. *Leysen*

The Green-cheeked Amazon *(Amazona viridigenalis)* is widely known among bird fanciers as the Mexican Red Head. This attractive bird is similar to Finsch's, Salvin's and Lilacine Amazons. It makes a pleasant pet and is highly trainable. Good breeding results are possible under favorable conditions and the Red Head has even been hybridized with Double Yellowheads and Spectacled Amazons. *Leysen*

The Blue-cheeked Amazon or Dufresne's Amazon *(Amazona d. dufresniana)* is very rare both in the wild and in aviculture and is only found in a handful of zoos and private collections. This is a generally docile bird that has good potential as a mimic and talker. It was named in honor of the French naval officer Nicholas T.M. du Fresne.
Leysen

The St. Vincent's Amazon *(Amazona guildingii)* is an extremely rare, endangered species at present, due to a pair of natural disasters that so decimated the population throughout its habitat that the species has never fully regained its former strength. The St. Vincent's is a large, strikingly-colored bird and initial successes at captive breeding offer hope to save these beautiful parrots in the future. *Leysen*

The African Grey *(Psittachus erithacus)* is universally regarded as one of the psittacine family's most gifted talkers and mimics. This species has a good temperament, learns easily and breeds readily. African Greys have been kept for centuries and have made many friends for aviculture. *Leysen*

The Timneh Parrot *(Psittachus e. timneh)* is a subspecies of the African Grey and is readily distinguishable from the nominate form. In terms of temperament and the potential for speech, differences between the two birds are negligible. *Leysen*

Maximilian's Parrot *(Pionus m. maximiliani)* is another in the *Pionus* genus and is characterized by small size, pleasant personality and freedom from the tendency for destructive behavior noted in many other parrot species. This bird also carries the interesting alternative name, Scaly-headed Parrot. This species is from Brazil. *Leysen/Vriends*

The Palm Cockatoo's bare cheek patches are capable of changing color according to the bird's mood.
Leysen/Vriends

be approximately 30 years old. For three successive years the pair always raised one young. Sydney's Taronga Zoo had a pair that were housed in an aviary, almost completely constructed of concrete, of 22½ x 7½ x 6 feet. The pair had a nestbox 4½ feet high and 15 inches in diameter; in the nest a thin layer of wood chips was placed. The nest-hollow was approximately 12 inches deep. The birds themselves carried quite an amount of nesting material to the box. After some time a porous, 2-inch layer accumulated. In the wild, the birds also take care that their nest will be porous, in the event of heavy rainfalls. In September the female disappeared into the box and on the 3rd of November one could hear the first chicks calling. The estimated incubation period was approximately 31 to 35 days. During the whole breeding process the male never entered the box but fed his bride through the nest opening. Unfortunately he fell sick in January to *Candida albicans* infection (a crop infection) so that parents and young had to be administered *Mycortatine* to cure them, which was successful. It still took about two months before the young birds were cured; however they died in April, 1972 of *psittacosis.* The Neuwied Zoo in Western Germany was more successful and raised a young bird in 1975.

Family: *Psittacidae*

The species of this family do not possess a crest; only a few representatives have a somewhat elongated crown and nape feathers.

177

Subfamily: *Nestorinae*

Noteworthy are the bristle-like feathers and the tongue, which is tipped with a hair-like fringe (Forshaw).

Genus: *Nestor* (Keas)

A stocky bird with a short tail and a long upper mandible.

Kea *Nestor notabilis* Gould

DESCRIPTION: This avicultural rarity is predominantly brownish-green in color, with dark edges to the feathers; the outer webs of the primaries are blue. The under-wing coverts are orange-red; the undersides of the flight feathers are yellow with an orange tinge; back and rump are orange-red. Beak brown-gray (the female's beak is not as long, and more curved). The iris of both sexes is dark brown; legs and feet are dark gray. Immature birds have yellowish green crowns; the eyelid and cere are yellow, as are their legs and feet, and the base of the lower mandible (Forshaw).

LENGTH: 19 inches (48 cm)

DISTRIBUTION: This mountain bird (up to 1800-6000 feet) comes from New Zealand's South Island. It is still very common, and lives on roots, buds, fruits, seeds, berries, blossoms and nectar. Keas are also found along rivers, on grassland and in forests. These highly intelligent, playful birds are not shy, like to roll in the snow, and even enter deserted huts and such, via windows or chimneys, in order to obtain some food!

SPECIAL NOTES: The birds eat practically everything they can lay their beaks on; they even like insects and their larvae and even carrion. They have a reputation as sheep-killers, which is untrue, and merely an exaggeration, although it is possible that they may attack sick or injured sheep trapped in the snow.

Keas must be kept in large aviaries where one can enjoy their huge jumps. It is necessary that the aviary has a rock with running water.

Another avicultural rarity is the Kaka (*Nestor medidionalis*), also from New Zealand, and some offshore islands. If you can secure a pair of these beautiful birds, be sure to offer them nectar and pollen, as well as insects and grubs. It is a pity that because of the loss of forest habitat the Kaka is declining in numbers drastically.

The female incubates the three to four eggs for 28 days, but both sexes feed their young, which fledge the nest after approximately two to 2½ months. Apart from the above-mentioned foods, sunflower seeds, corn, peanuts, lettuce, pumpkin seeds, berries and fruits are essential, as are canary seeds, millet, spray millet, brown bread, oats, wheat, green foods and other vegetables.

The Kea *(Nestor notabilis)*, is regarded by some as a curiosity in the parrot tribe. A native of New Zealand, the Kea has an unfortunate reputation as a sheep killer. Like most parrots, however, this unusual bird makes a pleasant, highly amusing pet.

Vriends

Genus: *Psittrichas*

The only member of this genus, Pesquet's Parrot, is striking for its small, vulture-like head and beak. There are no feathers on the brow or the face.

The bird was discovered in 1863. This species, presumably related to *Calyptorhynchus*, is one of the most primitive parrots now living. Therefore it is probably one of the most interesting and desirable birds for aviculturists too! They are, however, seldom seen in private collections. Well-known are the birds to be seen at the World of Birds Exhibit at the Bronx Zoo (New York). They may also be admired at the Wassenaars Zoo (The Hague, Holland), and Walsrode (Germany). The San Diego Zoo has a single specimen.

Pesquet's Parrot *Psittrichas fulgidus* (Lesson)

DESCRIPTION: Bristle-like neck-feathers. Predominantly deep black-brown, with red on the abdomen and wings. Black bill, naked black skin around the eyes and beak (face). Males have a red spot adjacent to the eye.

LENGTH: 20 inches (50 cm)

DISTRIBUTION: Central New Guinea, to an altitude of 6000 feet. According to the late Dr. Lendon, there is a possibility that these birds may also live on Cape York (Australia), as black-and-red-colored birds were seen frequently. It could very well be true that there are Pesquet's Parrots on Cape York, as the habitat there consists of tropical rain forests; individuals have observed many different bird species there that may also be found in New Guinea.

In the wild, these noisy birds live on fruits, berries, figs and blossoms. They live in pairs or small flocks, like to sit for hours on a branch of a dead tree, regardless of rain or shine, and they don't climb from branch to branch, as other Cockatoos do.

SPECIAL NOTES: According to Mr. J. Dochters van Leeuwen (Holland) the birds like to occupy the hollow trunk of a fruit tree. This aviculturist received a pair in 1975; at the end of 1976 the birds commenced inspecting the 24-inch-high trunk. It is interesting to note that all nesting materials were taken from the nest by the female; she tucked these between her feathers, in the same manner as Lovebirds do. The first egg was laid on January 21, the second three days later. After an incubation-time of 26 to 29 days the first egg was hatched (February 19, 1977). The male did not participate in the brooding process, although he foraged for his bride on the nest. On February 28th the male commenced feeding the chicks as well. At first the young were covered with a white-yellowish down, but by March 11th this down had turned black; at this point the female refused to warm her young any longer. After March 24th she no longer stayed on the nest at night. On May 5th, the young started to look out of the nestbox, produced some singing notes on May 7th, and left the nest on May 13th. It was primarily the male that foraged for the chicks.

After the first of August he even fed through the mesh, when the chicks were placed in an adjacent aviary. On November 21st, the female produced a new egg, two days later followed by a second one. Although one egg hatched, the chick died 12 weeks later, due to a fungus infection.

Family: *Loridae* (Lories and Lorikeets)

Characteristic are their glossy plumage and clamorous behavior. The birds live in groups, usually high up in the trees, looking for pollen, fruits, and nectar. The tongue has elongated papillae on the tip which become erect when feeding, for "harvesting pollen and pressing it into a form suitable for swallowing" (Forshaw). In captivity the birds feed on milk- and honey-soaked rusks, pure honey, a good vitamin-preparation, berries, fruits, germinated seeds and a good brand of baby food made of fruits and vegetables. Understandably, during hot days, it is better to soak the bread in water than in milk. There are also commercial foods on the market made especially for these birds. Food should be offered on a feeder of approximately 5 feet high, as Lories and Lorikeets don't like to forage on the ground.

Genus: *Chalcopsitta*

There is no sexual dimorphism; male and female are not to be distinguishable externally. The birds are of medium size, with a long, rounded tail. The naked skin surrounding the base of the lower mandible is characteristic (Forshaw).

In the colder states it is necessary to keep the birds indoors during fall and winter. Besides the above mentioned foods (see *Family*) the birds need sunflower seeds, a variety of nuts and fruits, different kinds of millet, canary seeds and oats.

Black Lory *Chalcopsitta atra* (Scopoli)

DESCRIPTION: Predominantly black, with a deep purple tinge; the rump is also purple. The underside of the tail is yellowish-green, with red. Beak and cere are black, feet and legs gray. The iris is reddish. Immature birds possess an almost white cere; the iris is still dark brown.

LENGTH: 13 inches (32 cm)

DISTRIBUTION: New Guinea and adjacent islands. There are four subspecies:
1. *C. a. atra,* from the Western portion of the Vogelkop (West Irian) and the islands of Batanta and Salawati;
2. *C. a. bernsteini,* from the island of Misool; the bird has red feathers instead of purple ones; especially noticeable on the head and thighs;
3. *C. a. insignis,* from the eastern portion of the Vogelkop, on the island of Amberpon, and on the Onim and Bomberai Peninsulas. This subspecies has even more red in its feathers and a blue-gray color on the head;

4. *C. a. spectabilis,* a subspecies from the Mamberich Peninsula, and probably an intermediate between *C. a. insignis* and *C. s. sintillata* (Yellow-streaked Lory).

All species and subspecies live along the edges of forests, on savannahs, open grassland and such. They bicker a lot and prefer to perch high up in the trees.

SPECIAL NOTES: One of the first breeding successes occurred in 1910 (Mr. E. J. Brooks). Two round eggs were laid. After a week the birds started to incubate the eggs of which one was hatched after approximately three weeks. After two months the chick left the nestbox.

It is advisable to keep imported birds indoors at 68° F (20° C) for the first year; they are susceptible to colds and drafts. During the night the birds must have a closed night shelter of comfortable temperature.

During the mating and breeding period these birds can be quite aggressive; therefore I suggest that pairs be kept in separate aviaries.

Similar to the above-named Lory are:
1. Duivenbode's Lory (*C. duivenbodei*), from the northern coast of western New Guinea;
2. Yellow-streaked Lory *(C. s. sintillata),* from southern New Guinea, and the Aru Islands;
3. Cardinal Lory (*C. cardinalis*), from Feni, Nissan, Lavongai, Tanga, Likir, and the Tabor Group, and the Solomon Islands; according to Forshaw this beautiful bird has recently colonized the Ontong Java atoll in the Solomon Islands.

Duivenbode's Lory is predominantly olive-brown, with yellow streaks, a yellow forehead and throat and yellow thighs; the rump is deep purple; the Yellow-streaked Lory is green, with yellow streaks on neck, breast and abdomen; the thighs are red, as are the fore-neck and under tail-coverts; the Cardinal Lory is red, with dark brown wings and back.

Personally I offer my Lories the following "porridge," prepared in two-quart plastic containers:

One part fruit pulp made of apple, pear, strawberries, pineapple, carrots and cucumber; I do not use bananas and oranges, as they cause indigestion;

One part rice flour, universal food for soft-billed birds, and equal parts of wheat, oats, rye and buckwheat-flour.

All this is mixed in a blender; then I add a cup of rose-hips syrup, half a cup of seaweed, a dessert spoon with a multivitamin, a cup of glucose, and 3 cups of pure honey. To this whole mixture I add water, till I get the thickness of yoghurt. I offer the birds enough for one day; the rest is refrigerated. During warm weather change such foods in the afternoon. Birds like fruits and willow-twigs too, some will even eat sunflower seeds and spray millet. Birds must also receive fresh drinking and bathing water daily, as well as fresh greens, such as lettuce and chickweed, grapes, raisins and other subtropical fruits. Half-ripe corn on the cob will often be appreciated.

Black Lory *(Chalcopsitta atra)*

Red Lories *(Eos bornea)*

Blue-Streaked Lory *(Eos reticulata)*

183

Rainbow Lory *(Trichoglossus haematodus)*

Edwards' Lory *(Trichoglossus haematodus capistratus)*

Chattering Lory *(Lorius garrulus)*

Yellow-backed Lory *(Lorius garrulus flavopalliatus)*

One remark in conclusion: don't make the porridge too thick. The birds have a habit of putting their beaks deep into the food. During warm weather crusts may be formed around and on the beak, which in turn can lead to fungus infections.

Genus: *Eos* (Red Lories)

Violet-Necked Lory *Eos squamata* Bonaparte

DESCRIPTION: The bird is predominantly red, with a purple neck and crown; the top part of the breast is purple-blue, as are the abdomen and the rest of the underside. The beak is yellowish red; the iris yellow or orange-red (brown in the female!); legs and feet are gray. The females are deeper in color than the males, especially the undersides of their bodies. Hens are smaller than males.

LENGTH: 10 inches (25 cm)

DISTRIBUTION: Northern Moluccas, Weda Island and the western Papuan Islands.
There are four subspecies:
1. *E. s. squamata*;
2. *E. s. riciniata*;
3. *E. s. atrocaerulea* and
4. *E. s. obiensis.*
Their courtship-dance is especially worth watching. The male circles his bride with fanned-out tail feathers.

SPECIAL NOTES: This extremely expensive Lory is regularly available. The female lays two eggs, and after approximately 60 days the chicks leave the nest, but will still be fed for another two to three weeks by both parents.

Red Lory *Eos bornea* (Linné)

DESCRIPTION: A predominantly red bird, it shows a little blue on undertail-coverts and lower tertials. The beak is orange-yellow; the iris is red, feet and legs are dark gray. Young birds have blue feather-edges and, if still very young, black beaks.

LENGTH: 12 inches (30 cm)

DISTRIBUTION: Amboina, Ceram and the Moluccas.

SPECIAL NOTES: This beautiful bird is not difficult to purchase; the price is relatively low. There are four different subspecies, but the differences are very subtle. The birds become tame very quickly, and will occasionally breed.
The same may be said of the Blue-streaked Lory (*E. reticulata*), originally from the Tanimbar Islands, but also from the Kai and Damar Islands, where they were introduced.

The Red-collared Lorikeet (*Trichoglossus haematodus rubritorquis*), from northern Australia and Queensland, is one of the 21 subspecies of the brilliantly-colored Rainbow Lory.

186

Both birds like to breed in a warm temperature; the incubation period is approximately 23 to 25 days. After nine weeks the chicks leave the nest. Offer boxes of 14 x 14 x 18 inches (18 inches represents the height); situate the box in a high place.

Genus: *Trichoglossus* (Wedgetailed Lories)

These medium-sized birds are known for their gradated tails. There is no sexual dimorphism. Their pointed wings enable them to fly swiftly; it is therefore understandable that these birds, more than others, need an aviary measuring at least 10½ feet in length. Too long a flight seems to make the birds very nervous and shy, so such quarters should be avoided.

All Lories like to roost in a large nest, and starling boxes can be used very nicely for this purpose. These must be cleaned out regularly due to the nature of the Lory's diet and character of the droppings.

Rainbow Lory *Trichoglossus haematodus* (Linné)

DESCRIPTION: This well-known bird is predominantly green, with a black-colored head with purple feathers; the neck is yellow; throat and breast are red with purple feather-edges; the belly is dark purple-blue, the feathers on the thighs are yellow, but have green edges. The beak is red. The iris of the male is red, that of the hen orange-red and color of the hen's breast is not as bright.

LENGTH: 13 to 14 inches (33-35 cm), depending on the subspecies.

DISTRIBUTION: Ceram, Moluccas, Amboina, Flores, Sumba, Bali, Lombok, New Guinea and eastern Australia.
There are 21 subspecies:
1. *T. h. haematodus* (Moluccas, Ceram, Amboina, Flores, Bali etc.; see above;
2. *T. h. mitchellii* (Bali and Lombok);
3. *T. h. forsteni* (Sumbawa);
4. *T. h. djampeanus* (Djampea Island);
5. *T. h. stresemanni* (Kalao tua);
6. *T. h. fortis* (Sumba);
7. *T. h. weberi* (Flores);
8. *T. h. capistratus* (Timor);
9. *T. h. rosenbergii* (Biak);
10. *T. h. flavotectus* (Wetar and Roma);
11. *T. h. intermedius* (northern West Irian and Manam Island);
12. *T. h. micropteryx* (West Irian and Misima Island);
13. *T. h. caeruleiceps* (southern West Irian);
14. *T. h. nigrogularis* (Aru Islands and eastern Kai Islands);
15. *T. h. brooki* (Spirit Islands (?) and Aru Islands);
16. *T. h. massena* (Bismarck Archipelago, Solomon Islands and the New Hebrides);

17. *T. h. flavicans* (New Hanover and the Admiralty Islands);
18. *T. h. nesophilus* (Ninigo Islands);
19. *T. h. deplanchii* (New Caledonia and the Loyalty Islands)
20. *T. h. moluccanus* (predominantly in eastern Australia, but also on Kangaroo Island, southern Australia and Tasmania);
21. *T. h. rubritorquis* (northern Australia, Kimberley to Queensland).

Of this species the following parrot is of special interest to us, as he is often available: the Swainson's or Blue Mountain Lory (*T. h. moluccànus*). This hardy, active bird frequently breeds. It will eat sunflower seeds, oats, white seed, spray millet, buckwheat, as well as nectar, pieces of apple, grapes and carrots fed daily. It is best to keep the birds in pairs in separate flights to avoid quarreling.

The display of the male during the courtship is interesting to watch; it consists of a weaving, swaying motion accompanied by a rustling sound. The two eggs are incubated for 25 days. The males only assist in feeding the young. It is possible to have more than one brood per season. Mr. W. de Grahl states that these birds are not fussy about where they breed, using any box that would suit a starling or woodpecker, with an entrance hole of approximately 3 inches in diameter. It is necessary to deposit an inch or so of wood shavings or peat moss on the bottom. Hand-reared specimens can be very affectionate and tame!

Genus: *Lorius*

These medium-sized birds have a short tail and broad bill. There is no sexual dimorphism.

Black-Capped Lory *Lorius lory* (Linné)

DESCRIPTION: The male has a black cap; the sides of the head are red; the throat, the nape band, the side of the body and the underwing coverts are red also; the wings are green; the remaining parts of the body are blue. The female is slimmer and possesses a smaller beak. The beak is orange-yellow; the iris orange-red or orange-yellow; feet and legs are dark gray.

LENGTH: Approximately 12 inches (31 cm)

DISTRIBUTION: West Irian and adjacent islands.
There are seven subspecies; all are rarely seen in aviculture.

SPECIAL NOTES: This attractive species is not regularly imported, is fairly expensive and seldom breeds. There are some tame birds on the market, though, that were originally reared by natives. These birds are very good imitators, and behave in a calm and dignified manner. I have known birds that could perform small tricks and were able to "play dead," on their backs. Without a daily supply of nectar it is impossible to keep the birds alive. They must also have soft fruits, cooked corn on the cob, and wheat. During the

The Chattering Lory (*Lorius g. garrulus*), an outstandingly gorgeous species, is found in Halmahera and the Weda Islands (Indonesia). Although they do well in colder climates when properly acclimated, they are better suited to aviary life than as cage birds.

winter months they must be housed in warm surroundings. A nestbox as a sleeping place is absolutely necessary.

Chattering Lory *Lorius garrulus* (Linné)

DESCRIPTION: Predominantly red, with a yellow triangular patch on the back. The wings are green, the bend of the wing is yellow. The beak is orange-yellow, the iris brown or yellowish-red; legs and feet are gray. When the birds are fully colored there are always some green feathers in the yellow back patch.

LENGTH: 12 inches (30 cm)

DISTRIBUTION: Halmahera and several surrounding islands. There are three subspecies of which the Yellow-backed Lory (*L. g. flavopalliatus*), from Batjan and Obi, is the costliest; it has a yellow back. The *L. g. morotaianus,* from Morotai and Raou, has a duller back-patch, and is a smaller bird.

SPECIAL NOTES: The Chattering Lory is the most common Lory. Watch out when dealing with these birds, as they are easily excited when strangers come near their aviaries. They then start to screech, are upset for hours and will even leave their brood unattended for quite some time.

In addition to the normal Lory menu, they need daily feedings of willow twigs, some greens such as chickweed, unripe weed-seeds and, especially, endive. They also need a proper night shelter in which a large nestbox is situated in an aviary at least nine feet long. When the birds are properly acclimatized they can remain in their aviary winter and summer. The female lays two eggs, that are incubated for approximately 24 days. Only the female sits on the eggs, although the male "gives her a hand" during the night. Don't be too alarmed when you see the female leave the nest for what appears a disturbingly long time. She is looking around for food and such behavior occurs regularly. There is nothing to worry about as long as she doesn't engage in this every day for hours on end.

Genus: *Deroptyus* (Hawk-headed Parrots)

Hawk-Headed Parrot *Deroptyus accipitrinus* (Linné)

DESCRIPTION: Dark salmon-pink with blue feather-edges. The feathers on the face white with blue edges; brow and crown snow-white. Green wings, thighs and undertail-coverts. Tail dark green, with a purple shade. Beak gray-black; iris yellow; feet and legs gray.

LENGTH: 14 inches (35 cm)

DISTRIBUTION: Northern areas of South America, eastern Venezuela, Guyana to Ecuador and the Amazon River basin.

SPECIAL NOTES: This is, as far as we know, the only parrot that is able to raise its head-feathers like a fan. The birds are rarities in aviculture, although in the

The Hawk-Headed Parrot (*Deroptyus accipitrinus*), a South American species, is the only known parrot with the ability to raise its head feathers to form a fan or ruff. He is a rarity in aviculture, but there have been captive breedings of this interesting, good natured bird. *Photo by Arthur Freud from ALL ABOUT THE PARROTS © 1980 by Arthur Freud, and reproduced with the permission of the publisher, Howell Book House Inc.*

1970s many successful breedings were accomplished in Germany, England and the United States of America.

For housing and feeding refer to the Amazon Parrots.

Genus: *Eclectus* (Eclectus Parrots)

Grand Eclectus *Eclectus roratus* (Linné)

DESCRIPTION: As both the sexes are totally different in color it was thought for a very long time that they were two species, until Dr. A. B. Meijer, of the National Museum of Natural History (Munich, Germany), discovered in 1874 that the males are predominantly green and the females red.

LENGTH: 14 inches (35 cm)

DISTRIBUTION: Moluccas, Ceram, Amboina, Sumba, Halmahera, Solomon Islands, New Guinea and adjacent islands, and northern Queensland, in ten subspecies.

SPECIAL NOTES: These birds need daily: cooked rice, germinated and dry sunflower seeds, in milk-soaked bread and/or rusk, sweet fruits, raisins, berries, flower-buds, lettuce, dandelion, spinach and chickweed.

Imported birds must be housed in warm 68° F (20° C) indoor aviaries (only one pair per aviary), and they must be given the opportunity to drink fresh water whenever they like. The birds rarely breed and when they do the female lays two eggs which she hatches in 28 days. Use boxes of 12 inches x 12 inches x 20 inches, with an entrance of 6 inches in diameter (20 inches represents the height).

Genus: *Agapornis* (Lovebirds)

Lovebirds got their name because of their affectionate natures, although the females of the Black-winged Lovebird and the Gray-headed Lovebird are the dominant sex, as they select the nest site and defend this against other birds. They even snap at their mates. Mutual preening of these two species is rather one-sided.

Lovebirds are delightful animals, whether kept in a roomy cage or a large aviary. Generally speaking, they breed quite readily and capture one's heart with their adorable chatter. In the wild they often nest in loose colonies, and one tree may shelter many nests.

They are found in the tropical parts of Africa, and on the island of Madagascar. *Agapornis* species are recognized by their short, rounded tails. On the average, the birds are about five to six inches long. Although most of their plumage is green, we have recognized species which have some yellow, red and blue feathers. Lovebirds live in small groups in forests, plains and swamps; some species live in mountainous regions up to approximately 9000 feet above sea level; others frequent the open fields, but all species in this genus can be found south of 13 degrees north latitude.

Grand Eclectus Parrots *(Eclectus roratus)* come from Australia, New Guinea and several islands of the South Pacific. It is believed that this species was once held sacred by the natives in part of its habitat. This was probably because of its strikingly beautiful color and markings.

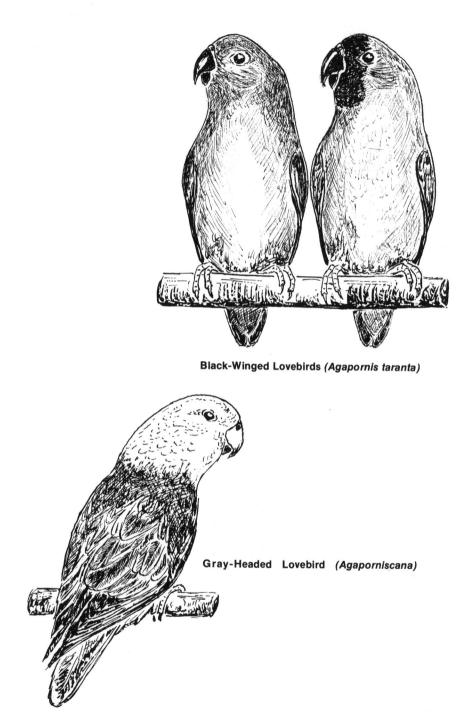

Black-Winged Lovebirds *(Agapornis taranta)*

Gray-Headed Lovebird *(Agaporniscana)*

194

Agapornis species feed on various types of grass seeds, sweet berries, fruit, and a variety of grains and grass; in captivity they should be offered a number of different seeds, as well as groats, dry and water-soaked rice, berries, millet, new green twigs, egg, melba toast, other fruit such as bananas, orange sections, sweet apple pieces, cherries, pears, soaked raisins and currants, "ant's eggs" and the so-called universal foods. In addition, the birds should be offered cuttlefish bone and oyster grit daily.

Agapornis species use nesting materials; in fact, they use quite a lot to construct their nests. Several species even transport these building materials in between their back and/or chest feathers. Lovebirds live and breed in colonies, although during the breeding period some will break away into small groups to share the "good and bad" together. Even in these smaller groups some disharmony might occur, but to a lesser degree than in the larger colony. In each colony, one of the stronger males will act as leader to intervene successfully if and when little "disagreements" present themselves. This will take place even in an aviary housing several couples of one particular kind. I have observed that these minor arguments are mostly restricted to evening quarrels, for rarely will these birds steal nesting material or food from each other; in any event, their breeding habits are rarely affected by these little upsets.

Black-Winged Lovebird *Agapornis taranta* (Stanley)

DESCRIPTION: Both sexes are grass green; the male has a red brow. The periophthalmic ring is also red, greenish in the female. The tail is black tipped. The feathers just below the tail show a yellow glow, as does the curve of the wings. Rump and feathers immediately above the tail are light green, as is the entire top of the bird; the underside is light green also. The feathers under the wings are black; in females greenish, sometimes brownish-black. Immature birds look like their mother, except for the beak which will remain brownish-yellow until a few weeks later, when it will turn red. The iris of the adult bird is brown.

LENGTH: 6 to 6.5 inches (15-16.5 cm)

DISTRIBUTION: Southern Eritrea and southwestern Ethiopia. There are two subspecies:
   1. *A. t. taranta;* this bird is a little larger than:
   2. *A. t. nana;* this subspecies has shorter wings and a small bill.
   Black-winged Lovebirds generally live together in small groups. The nest is used as a year-round roost, making the population rather stationary. Their singing is not at all offensive, apart from the occasional little screeching notes they tend to include in their song once in awhile. If they are upset they may even give voice to it at night! Their song is soft, but should not be compared to that of song birds. They prefer the sparse woods of the highlands, and sometimes can be found at a height of 6000 to 9000 feet above sea level. Consequently, they are accustomed to some cold weather and can be kept in the

195

outside aviary even during the winter, providing there is a draft-free and dry night shelter available. It is desirable to hang a few nesting boxes in the shelter as Lovebirds prefer to sleep in these.

SPECIAL NOTES: The female lays between three to six white eggs; they are laid every other day. Depending upon the weather it will take 24 to 26 days for the eggs to hatch. *Tarantas* seldom build a nest; I provide a thick layer of moist wood-shavings which I press down firmly. The nesting box measures 10 inches long x 6 inches deep x 7 inches high—these are inside measurements. It is advisable to separate the young from their parents once they have become adults to avoid accidents.

Peach-Faced Lovebird *Agapornis roseicollis* (Vieillot)

DESCRIPTION: The male has a soft pinkish-red forehead, cheeks, chin, throat, as well as an area just above the chest; the forehead being the darkest. Most of the rest is bright green, the underside being lighter with a hint of yellow. Rump and covering feathers above the tail bright light blue, while on the green tail there are some black and rust-colored feathers. The eyes are brown, the beak is yellow to very light green and the feet and legs are greenish-gray. There is a faint ring around the eyes. The female is difficult to determine; the green and blue colors and particularly the orange in the tail are considerably less sharp than the male's colors, although the beak is darker in color; in spite of these small differences, it is still hard to see the difference between male and female. Immature birds are grayish-green, and lack the red coloring on the forehead.

LENGTH: 6 to 7 inches (16-18 cm). It is the largest of the Lovebirds.

DISTRIBUTION: This bird is an inhabitant of Benguela, a region in Angola, Africa. In the wild they live in comparatively small groups.
  There are two subspecies:
  1. *A. r. roseicollis,* which was probably discovered and documented by about 1817;
  2. *A. r. catumbella,* discovered in 1955 and recognized by its brighter colors.

SPECIAL NOTES: The Peach-faced Lovebird is supposedly the first species to have been seen transporting nest-building materials between its back and rump feathers. The female lays four to five eggs. After 30 to 38 days the young fly out of the nest but will continue to be fed (mostly by the father) for some time, while the mother starts laying new eggs or looks for a new nesting box.
  The correct diet for these birds, when kept in a roomy aviary, consists of millet, canary seed, buckwheat, hemp, linseed, cracked sunflower seeds, fresh twigs (from willow, beech, hazel, elderberry, pine, pear, apple and common privet trees, for example) and fruit. Unfortunately, not many of these species like fruit, which is a shame as I have noticed that those that do eat fruit tend to have more shiny and healthy looking plumage. Offering them a variety of

fruits may encourage more of your pets to try it. Small pieces of apple or pear, pineapple, sliced figs, soaked currants or raisins and various berries are all suitable. Don't forget sunflower seeds and hemp; the hemp should be offered only in small quantities; one teaspoon per day is more than sufficient. Once the young have left the nest, this can be increased to two teaspoons per day. Incidentally, an excellent food for the baby birds is eggs with rusks. Don't give too many oil-containing seeds, since this will promote feather picking. Offer all kinds of greens, such as lettuce, endive and chickweed, but don't expect them to attack the greens with fervor or you will be disappointed. They do, however, prefer greens to fruit.

To date there are a number of color mutations.

Gray-Headed Lovebird *Agapornis cana* (Gmelin)

DESCRIPTION: The entire head, cheeks, throat and neck and parts of the shoulders and chest are whitish-gray. The underparts are light grass-green; the wings are dark green; the tail is green with black tips. The chest has a hazy yellow glow which becomes darker towards the wings and the underside. The beak is whitish-gray, the legs and feet are gray and the eyes are brown. The female is predominantly green. Whereas the undersides of the wings in the male are black, those of the female are green. Immature birds can be sexed at an early age. The young males are a more intense green on the back and wings, and the gray can be seen quite early in life, sometimes while they are still in the nest. The beaks of the females are generally lighter than those of the males.

LENGTH: 5½ inches (14 cm)

DISTRIBUTION: Madagascar and adjacent islands. There are two subspecies:
1. *A. c. cana* and
2. *A. c. ablectanea;* this subspecies is only found in the southwest region of Madagascar. The "trademark" of this bird is the brighter gray colors of its head, neck and chest, and the sharper greens of its wings and underside.

Gray-headed Lovebirds often travel in large flocks of 150 or more birds, often causing considerable damage to farmland. They live mostly along the edge of forests where there are trees that shed their leaves. The birds use shallow holes in trees as well as crevices in rocks and other places to build their nests, with tree holes being the most popular and common. The female lays from four to six white eggs, and in the wild I have seen nests that contained as many as 8, 9 and 11 eggs.

SPECIAL NOTES: Only when these birds are kept in a roomy aviary will they breed, although even then there are no guarantees. Acclimatization of the birds is most important; for these birds can still present problems before they have adjusted to their new lodging and become comfortable with their environment.

There have been no color mutations reported with this species.

Red-Faced Lovebird *Agapornis pullaris* (Linné)

DESCRIPTION: The male is predominantly green, darker on top than underneath where often a yellowish glow can be seen. The forehead, cheeks and throat are tomato-red and the beak is scarlet. The narrow ring around the eye is white, yellow or bluish in color. The rump is sky blue, but the covering feathers just above the tail are green. The primary flight feathers have black tips; the curve of the wings is black with blue. The center tail feathers are green while the rest of the tail feathers are red with a black band a little before the tips, but the tips themselves are green. Feet and legs are greenish-gray and the covering feathers under the wings are black. The female's face is orange rather than tomato-red, and this colored area is usually smaller than the male's. The covering feathers under the wings are green. The immature birds resemble the female, although the covering feathers under the wings quickly become black in the young males. The bill is orange-red with a yellow tip.

LENGTH: 6 inches (15 cm)

DISTRIBUTION: Although not all authors agree, most divide this species into two subspecies, namely:
1. *A. p. pullaria,* a native of West Africa and the Gold Coast, and
2. *A. p. ungandae,* from Uganda and Ruanda.

SPECIAL NOTES: This species carves its nest in the large, still-inhabited tree nest of termites, or in termite hills; the average size of such a nest is approximately 12 to 24 inches high. They have comparatively hard exterior walls encasing an interior of several tunnels with much more permeable walls. The substance of which this structure is made consists primarily of termite feces bonded with saliva, which becomes quite firm after it dries. Lovebirds of this species have also been known to make nests in uninhabited termite "castles."

In an aviary, it was noted that a female gnawed green leaves from the shrubbery, placed them between her feathers and flew into her nest with them; it has also been noted that the female will use small pieces of willow twigs, if they are made available. The best breeding results are obtained by using corkboards and securely affixing these in a tree trunk; the same dimensions should be followed as those for a regular nesting box. Recently man has tried to imitate building the termite nests by filling a 44-gallon drum with peat-moss; the peat-moss was wet down before it was put in the drum, and then left to dry. The drum was opened at one end and placed in the direction of the flight. Branches and twigs were arranged on top and around it to give it a "natural" appearance. Before long the birds started digging; it is noteworthy that no nesting material was used, and that the eggs and later the young laid on top of the hard mulch. Normally this species lays between four and seven eggs. The female does the hatching, while the male provides her with food.

Masked Lovebird *Agapornis p. personata* Reichenow

DESCRIPTION: Blackish-brown head with yellow collar. Throat and chest are

Masked Lovebird *(Agapornis p. personata)*

Fischer's Lovebird *(Agapornis p. fischeri)*

yellow with an orange-red glow. The balance of the body is primarily green with the exception of the rump, which is bluish, and the tail, which shows a black and red band shortly before the ends on the outer feathers. The brown eyes are encircled with a wide, white periophthalmic ring; the legs are gray. The females weigh about 2 ounces, the males slightly less.

LENGTH: 6 to 6¼ inches (15-15.7 cm)

DISTRIBUTION: Northeast Tanganyika, southeast of Lake Tanganyika.

SPECIAL NOTES: Nesting boxes should be large, measuring at least 20 x 10 inches. The construction of the nest itself is an action exclusive to the hen. I have kept three pairs together in one aviary a few times and provided them with ten nesting boxes to avoid quarreling and was rewarded with success. If it is a warm and sunny spring, hose off the nest boxes each morning and night, but take care that none of the water actually seeps inside. For more details see notes under GENUS.

There are quite a few color mutations, the blue mutation being the best known. The collar, chest and belly of this mutation are a sort of off-white, while the head is black. The beak is horn-colored.

Fischer's Lovebird *Agapornis p. fischeri* Reichenow

DESCRIPTION: The back, chest and wings are green; the neck is a golden yellow, while the cheeks and throat are orange. The top of the head is olive-green, the forehead is a lovely tomato-red. The feathers just above the tail are blue, the tail is green with sky-blue tips and with an indistinct black band shortly before the ends. The base of the outermost feathers of the wings are brownish-red underneath. The beak is red with a white curved line that runs along the top of the beak. There is also a similar white border around the eyes, which are brown. The legs are slate blue. Immature birds look like their parents except that their colors are somewhat duller, and the base of the mandible has brown markings.

LENGTH: 4 inches (10 cm)

DISTRIBUTION: South and southeast of Lake Victoria; East Africa north of Tanganyika.

SPECIAL NOTES: See notes under GENUS. An important color mutation is the blue variety. This mutation is somewhat smaller than the wild bird and has an extremely pale gray head. It was first bred by R. Horsham in South Africa around 1957. Two years later, in 1959, it was bred in San Francisco, California by Dr. F. B. Warford.

Nyasa Lovebird *Agapornis p. lilianae* Shelley

DESCRIPTION: Primarily green in color, the underside being a little lighter; the forehead and the crown are tomato-red while the cheeks and throat are paler, more of an orange-red color. The green tail has a yellowish tint at the base and a dark band shortly before the tip. The tail starts off green, but later ends up with a base that turns to an orange-red. The beak is red, the feet and legs are grayish-brown, and the iris is brown. The female is identical to the male, although sometimes the red on her head is a little less bright. Her eyes may be a shade lighter. There is also a slight weight difference between the sexes; the female weighing about 43 grams and the male about $1\frac{1}{4}$ ounce. The offspring is duller in color, with the green and red colors somewhat darker. The color of the cheeks is still a little vague.

LENGTH: $4\frac{1}{4}$ inches (11 cm)

DISTRIBUTION: Nyasaland and Northern Rhodesia. For more details see notes under GENUS.

Black-Cheeked Lovebird *Agapornis p. nigrigenis* Sclater

DESCRIPTION: This bird looks like the *A. p. lilianae,* but the forehead and cheeks are black, hence the name. Their brown eyes are encircled by a wide white periophthalmic ring. The feet are gray, the beak is red, being somewhat paler at its base. The rest of the body is primarily green, the underside being a little lighter. There is a vague pink blotch on the chest. The female is virtually identical to the male, although her colors tend to be a little duller. However, since there are often such variations between individual birds, one cannot rely on this slight difference. The young birds look very much like the parents, although in their early life their colors are considerably duller. Some fledglings have black spots on the beak.

LENGTH: $5\frac{3}{4}$ inches (14.5 cm)

DISTRIBUTION: The northern portion of Southern Rhodesia, around the Zambezi River and the Victoria Falls, where I had the opportunity to observe them in small groups. Although this bird is readily available on the market, in its natural environment it is being threatened by extinction if the authorities there do not make stricter laws to protect it. The species' habitat is relatively small, being only around 80 miles in diameter.

SPECIAL NOTES: For more details see notes on previous species and GENUS.

Genus: *Opopsitta* (Fig Parrots)

These brilliantly-colored birds are kept by specialists. They require the same care as *Agapornis, Loriculus* and *Forpus.* This genus includes:
1. Double-eyed Fig Parrot (*O. d. diopthalma*), from the western Papuan Islands, Mistol and Salawati; with a red forehead and cheeks, and at the end of the crown some orange feathers, bordered with a purple band. Length: $4\frac{3}{4}$ inches (12 cm).
2. Orange-breasted Fig Parrot (*O. gulielmiterti*), from the southern

portion of West Irian and the Aru Islands. The bird has a blue crown, and a yellow throat; the cheeks are bordered with black; the breast is red. Length: 4¾ inches (12 cm).

3. Ramsay Fig Parrot (*O. diophthalma macleayana*), from the coastal areas of southern Queensland and northern New South Wales. This species has a red spot on the forehead, and red cheeks. Blue around the eyes. The female lacks the red colors. Length: 6¼ inches (16 cm).

Genus: *Loriculus* (Hanging Parrots)

These charming small birds with a short tail and pointed little beaks are closely related to the well-known Lovebirds (*Agapornis*). They roost, like bats: upside down. The female carries nesting material tucked in the rump feathers, just like Lovebirds do. They forage on sweet berries, fruits and sugar cane, and nest in a tree-hollow, or even on the ground. The hen lays three to four eggs. The majority of imported birds are still immature and not fully colored. At first Hanging Parrots need to be housed in warm quarters; as soon as they have their adult plumage, they can be placed in an outdoor aviary. At that time one has usually discovered, to his big surprise, that practically all the birds are males! Personally I prefer to house these birds in indoor aviaries the year 'round at room temperature. I think breeding chances are much higher then.

The birds are very peaceful, and constantly on the move; they also love to climb. Keep this in mind when furnishing your aviaries.

Their voices, however, are far from enjoyable.

It is, further, advisable to plant reed and cane in the aviary, so that the birds' nails can be kept short naturally; regular check-ups on the growth of their nails, however, remains inevitable.

We offer pieces of sweet apple (apple sauce may be given as well), berries, small chunks of bananas, opened figs, cooked corn and rice, soaked raisins, in honey-soaked bread and/or rusk, ant's eggs, universal foods, germinated canary seed, oats and chopped hard-boiled egg; every other day give some sliced, boiled potato. I also suggest that you offer "baby" fruit juices as "drinking water."

Vernal Hanging Parrot *Loriculus vernalis* (Sparrman)

DESCRIPTION: Predominantly grass-green, with a blue patch on the throat; back and tail feathers are red. Tail feathers underneath bluish white. The female lacks the throat patch, and is predominantly yellowish-green. The beak is red, the iris whitish, legs and feet red. The immature birds don't have the throat patch as yet, and are generally dull gray-green.

LENGTH: 6¼ inches (16 cm)

DISTRIBUTION: Central and northern India and Thailand.

Blue-Crowned Hanging
Parrot *(Loriculus galgulus)*

SPECIAL NOTES: These lively birds live primarily in wooded areas, but also on cultivated land. When the trees are in bloom hundreds of these parrots can be seen in relatively small areas.

The birds can be kept in large cages of 32 x 24 x 32 inches (80 x 60 x 80 cm), or in birdrooms. Due to the nature of their diet, their droppings are in liquid form; therefore keep perches and shrubs away from the sides of the cage or birdroom, for obvious reasons.

So far only a few breeding successes are recorded. A Danish aviculturist had a pair that raised one chick. The pair bred in a cardboard nest box; the incubation period was 24 days. The nest was built from small strips of willow bark and reed stems. It is advisable to use the well-known Budgerigar breeding boxes.

Blue-Crowned Hanging Parrot *Loriculus galgulus* (Linné)

DESCRIPTION: This parrot is predominantly green; the crown is blue; throat and rump are red; the lower back is yellowish. The female has very little blue on the crown, and lacks all red and yellow on her throat and lower back. Immature birds look like the female, lack the red and blue colors, have a reddish brown rump and a horn-colored beak. The beak of the adult male is black; the iris dark brown, feet and legs orange-yellow.

LENGTH: 5 inches (13 cm)

DISTRIBUTION: Sumatra, Borneo and the Malay Peninsula.

203

SPECIAL NOTES: This Hanging Parrot is one of the most commonly-kept species. It breeds regularly; the first recorded instance was in 1907 in Germany.

The female lays three to four, sometimes only two eggs, that are incubated for approximately 21 days; the male feeds his bride on the nest and he later assists in foraging for his young, although for the first few days, only the female takes care of the feeding. After about a month the chicks leave the nest box. After a year the young are fully-colored.

A standard Budgerigar nest box will suit *L. galgulus* and it is advisable to remove and clean the nest box thoroughly after each breeding round. In warmer states these birds can be housed in outdoor aviaries, but each aviary must have a proper night-shelter. During the winter months they must be kept indoors, at a temperature of approximately 68° F (20° C).

Sometimes the Philippine Hanging Parrot (*L. philippensis*) is imported. This species has 11 subspecies. The bird is green, with a red brow and an orange throat; the cheeks are green. They have a beautiful golden-colored nape, and the beak is red. The lower throat of the female is yellowish-blue, her cheeks are blue and the brow is deep red. Immature birds are green, with a red rump. At first the beaks of the chicks are yellowish, the nape has quite a bit of yellow, and the brow is still yellowish-red.

In the wild they are primarily forest birds, live in pairs or small flocks, and forage for nectar (especially nectar from coconut trees), seeds, blossoms, berries and fruits.

Genus: *Forpus* (Parrotlets)

What Lovebirds are for Africa, Parrotlets are for South America. They are America's smallest parrots—4¾ to 5½ inches (12-14 cm); inhabiting wooded areas in colonies; they dislike dense rain forests. They forage for fruits, berries, seeds and, sometimes, even insects. During the breeding season they search for hollow trees or thick branches, but also for holes in the ground; quite often they even use old nests of the Ovenbird. The female lays three to seven eggs, sometimes more.

In captivity the birds remain shy for some time. In the colder states they must be kept indoors at room-temperature. Birds bred in this country are strong and very affectionate. Feed them canary seed, millet, spray millet, groats, the smallest sunflower seeds, pieces of sweet apple, figs, chickweed, sorrel, dandelion, and soaked white bread, together with pieces of hard-boiled egg and a good brand of universal food. Parrotlets eat a fair amount of all this, so keep enough food on hand.

Hand-raised Parrotlets make ideal pets; they have quiet voices and learn to speak, whistle, laugh, cough or sneeze. They breed in Budgerigar boxes, in which is placed a layer of peat moss and wood shavings. In the breeding period the female produces one egg every 35 to 38 hours, till the clutch is complete. The eggs will be incubated by the hen only; after 19 to 22 days they hatch.

During the female's breeding time the male sits near the nest entrance, watching intently what is going on around him; as soon as he detects danger he whistles a high-pitched call to warn his bride, who then leaves the nest. When the young are about one month old they leave the nest, but will still be fed by the parents for another 18-20 days.

Parrotlets are fine birds, that, as a rule, get along well with each other and with other bird species; personally I have kept them with several finches without difficulties. However, during the breeding season be cautious, as the male likes to nip at his neighbors.

Parrotlets bred in the United States can be safely housed indoors without heating during late fall and winter; in the summer months they may be kept in an outdoor aviary with a dry and, especially draft-free night shelter.

There are seven species:
1. Green-rumped Parrotlet (*F. passerinus*), with five subspecies, from Colombia, Venezuela, Guyana, Peru, Brazil and Paraguay. Length: 5 inches (13 cm).
2. Mexican Parrotlet (*F. cyanopygius*), with three subspecies, from northwestern Mexico and the Tres Marias Islands. Length: 5 inches (13 cm).
3. Sclater's Parrotlet (*F. sclateri*), with two subspecies, from eastern

Green-rumped Parrotlet *(Forpus passerinus)*

Red-browed Fig Parrot *(Opopsitta diopthalma macleayana)*

Double-eyed Parrot *(Opopsitta diopthalma diopthalma)*

Orange-breasted Fig Parrot *(Opopsitta gulielmiterti)*

Ecuador, eastern Peru and eastern Venezuela, Guyana and western Brazil. Length: 5 inches (12.5 cm).

4. Blue-winged Parrotlet (*F. xanthopterygius*), with six subspecies, from northwestern Colombia into central and north-east Peru to northern Brazil. Length: 4¾ inches (12 cm).
5. Spectacled Parrotlet (*F. conspicillatus*), with three subspecies, from eastern Panama, Colombia and western Venezuela. Length: 4¾ inches (12 cm).
6. Pacific Parrotlet (*F. coelestis*), from Ecuador and Peru. Length: 5 inches (12.5 cm).
7. Yellow-faced Parrotlet (*F. xanthops*), from northwestern Peru. Length: 5¾ inches (14.5 cm).

Genus: *Ara* (Macaws)

These impressive, colorful birds sometimes live at an altitude of 9,000 feet above sea level. During the breeding season they look for large tree cavities and frequently occupy the same nesting places from previous years. The natives are aware that Macaws come back to "where their old cradle stood," and pass this knowledge on to other members of their family, so that for many generations certain families know precisely where to find different nesting places.

Macaws have been popular for many centuries. In the past their feathers were used like money to pay debts, taxes, for food and other commodities, as well as for adornment. Natives still remove the young from the nest and hand-rear them. Later they are sold for a nice sum of money.

In the wild—where due to deforestation, populations are diminishing daily at a horrifying rate—Macaws feed on all sorts of seeds, fruits, berries, corn, flowers and crops. They can do much damage to plantations. It is most likely that Macaws mate for life, as the pairs stay together all year round, even after the breeding season, when sometimes large flocks are formed. It is interesting to know, that chicks not fed on time, and becoming hungry, commence tapping their beaks against the sides of the "maternity room" to let their parents know they would like to receive some food!

Macaws are well-known in the United States. The majority of the imported birds are still young and hand-reared. Macaws are highly intelligent birds that learn all sorts of tricks, and even a few words, in very little time. When properly cared for, they can grow to be very old; one hundred years and more is not spectacular!

The birds feed on all kinds of nuts, seeds, vegetables, corn on the cob, oats, wheat, apple, carrots, rusk, and willow and fruit-tree twigs and branches.

Macaws can be housed in a large cage of about 67 x 59 x 67 inches, on a stand, or in an outdoor aviary. Tame birds can be kept on stands, without a chain on one leg. If you must use a chain, be sure the size is correct and keep

The Scarlet Macaw *(Ara macao)*, big, colorful and a worldwide favorite.   *Ebben*

checking this as the bird grows; change the chain to the other leg every other day to prevent injuries and swelling.

One last word on breeding: Macaws, and certainly dwarf Macaws, regularly breed in captivity, if we make certain the pair is housed in a large aviary (at least 15 feet in length). The only problem we face is that it is unknown precisely when Macaws become sexually mature. Our only alternative is to wait! I have said it before: if you don't have enough patience, don't get involved in aviculture!

Scarlet Macaw *Ara macao* (Linné)

DESCRIPTION: Predominantly red, with yellow wings and shoulders; the tips of these yellow feathers are green. Naked white cheeks (that become pinkish, when the bird is upset or nervous). White-yellowish iris; upper mandible ivory, with black on the base; the lower mandible is gray-black. Legs and feet dark gray. Immature birds still have some green on the wing coverts, while the underwing coverts possess red and olive-yellow colors.

LENGTH: 31½ to 35½ inches; tail 20 to 24 inches (80-90 cm; tail 50-60 cm)

DISTRIBUTION: From Mexico to Peru.

SPECIAL NOTES: This species is a fair talker. Breeding results are regularly reported. The female needs a nest box of 24 inches in diameter; the nest hollow must have a layer of peat moss and wood chips of at least two inches. After three weeks the eggs hatch; after approximately 95 days the young leave the nest. At about five months the young are fully colored. Bananas, orange sections, tomatoes, soaked and dry bread, carrots, sunflower seeds, canary seeds. greens and oats are essential during the mating and breeding seasons.

Military Macaw *Ara militaris* (Linné)

DESCRIPTION: Both male and female are predominantly green, with a red forehead, blue rump and upper tail coverts. Characteristic are the four small rows of red feathers on the naked white cheeks. Iris yellow, beak black, feet and legs dark gray. Immature birds are duller, with a broad green edge on the nape.

LENGTH: 26 inches (65 cm)

DISTRIBUTION: Mexico to Argentina. This species lives in groups of approximately 40 birds in arid and semi-arid regions "up to 7500 feet altitude in pine and oak forests" (Forshaw).

SPECIAL NOTES: not as proficient a talker as the previous Macaw. For more details see notes under GENUS.

Severe Macaw *Ara severa* (Linné)

DESCRIPTION: The male of this dwarf Macaw is predominantly green, with a brownish-red forehead, and a red wing band. The primary feathers are blue, the blue tipped tail is reddish brown. Whitish cheeks with rows of small black feathers. Iris yellow, beak black, feet and legs gray. The female's brow is not as pronounced as the male's. Immature birds possess, until they are approximately six months old, a black iris.

LENGTH: 19 inches (48 cm)

DISTRIBUTION: Panama, Colombia, Ecuador and Bolivia. They live in forests and valleys, and are very common.

SPECIAL NOTES: This quiet bird becomes tame very quickly, and will learn to speak a few words. They often breed under favorable conditions; supply nest boxes of 16 x 16 x 30 inches with an entrance of five inches in diameter. In the nest some peat moss and wood chips are necessary; a layer of 1½ inches is advisable. The female incubates the three to five eggs, the male remains near the nest entrance, but disappears into the nest for the night. The incubation time is approximately 24 to 26 days. After eight weeks the chicks leave the nest; young males are distinguishable as they already have a red forehead. During mating and breeding time all kinds of nuts, rice, carrots, fruits, seeds, sprouted sunflower seeds and oats are necessary, along with pieces of hardboiled egg, twigs, lettuce, leaves, bread and universal foods.

Illiger's Macaw *Ara maracana* (Vieillot)

DESCRIPTION: The male and female of this group of dwarf Macaws are predominantly green. The male has a red forehead, lower back and V-shaped patch on the belly. The blue-tipped tail is brownish-red; the undertail feathers are yellowish-gray. The yellow cheeks have barely visible rows of small black feathers. The female's V-shaped belly-patch and brow are not as prominent as the male's. Immature birds lack or have a little red in their feathers, while their bellies are still pale green.

LENGTH: 17 inches (44 cm)

DISTRIBUTION: Eastern Brazil. This common Macaw inhabits forests, close to water.

SPECIAL NOTES: They breed readily: in the Whipsnade Zoo a pair reared ten chicks over a period of several years. The female incubates her two or three eggs for approximately 25 days. Use a nestbox of 18 x 14 x 30 inches, with an entrance of 6 inches in diameter. During the whole mating and breeding season the birds enjoy soaked bread and/or rusks, along with the foods mentioned in the notes under GENUS.

Blue and Gold Macaw *Ara ararauna* (Linné)

DESCRIPTION: Wings, back, rump and tail coverts blue, with a greenish haze. Forehead blue-green, lower parts and neck orange-yellow. On the white

210

The Severe Macaw *(Ara severa)*, is also known as the Chestnut-fronted Macaw. The alternate name is taken from the brown feathers that appear above the cere.   *Ebben*

The Military Macaw's *(Ara militaris)* natural habitat covers a very wide range and goes as far north as parts of central and western Mexico, making it the most northward ranging of all the larger New World parrots.

Illiger's Macaw *(Ara maracana)*, like many other species is threatened in the wild due to deforestation of its natural habitat. Fortunately, this dwarf Macaw breeds readily in captive situations.

cheeks are a few rows of small black feathers; throat black. Iris yellow, beak black, feet and legs dark gray.

LENGTH: 35½ inches (90 cm); the female is smaller than the male, especially in beak and head.

DISTRIBUTION: Eastern Panama to northern Paraguay. These birds are still common "in forests, in more remote parts of their range, but have declined in numbers or disappeared altogether from accessible regions" (Forshaw).

SPECIAL NOTES: These highly intelligent birds are very popular as pets, and breeding results are even obtained in large aviaries. A pair in the Magdeburg Zoo bred in an aviary of 11′6″ x 5′9″ x 7′10″, and used a nest box of 20 x 20 x 31 inches, with an entrance of 5½″ in diameter. The box was constructed from 1½ inch thick boards. The female produces two to three eggs that will be incubated for approximately 25 days. After 2½ months the chicks leave the nest. Mr. E. Kjelland (Chicago) had a pair that were housed in a cage (measuring 24 x 47 x 47 inches) which stood in a store! They bred in a metal box containing a layer of cedar shavings and wood chips. The first time the female laid two eggs, one of which was fertile. The second clutch consisted of three eggs; all eggs hatched, but one young died when it was only a couple of days old; the two surviving chicks were brought up by hand, as soon as they were completely feathered. Their favorite food was corn on the cob. For that matter the female loved it too!

Green-Winged Macaw *Ara chloroptera* (G. R. Gray)

DESCRIPTION: Predominantly red; the upper wing and shoulder coverts are dark green, the rest of the wing is blue. These birds very much resemble the *Ara macao*, but have rows of small red feathers on the white cheeks.

LENGTH: 35½ inches (90 cm)

DISTRIBUTION: Eastern Panama to Paraguay.

SPECIAL NOTES: In the wild these birds often hybridize with the Military Macaw, and with the Blue and Gold Macaw. For further details see notes under GENUS, and the section on the Blue and Gold Macaw.

Genus: *Anodorhynchus* (Hyacinth Macaws)

These beautiful, large birds are predominantly blue and have long gradated tails. The periophthalmic ring is yellow and prominent.

Hyacinth Macaw *Anadorhynchus hyacinthinus* (Latham)

DESCRIPTION: Predominantly cobalt-blue with dark gray on the under tail coverts. The periophthalmic ring is small and yellow. A small strip of yellow skin borders the lower mandible. The beak is dark gray, the iris dark brown, feet and legs dark gray.

The Blue and Gold Macaw (*Ara ararauna*), one of the world's most popular Macaw species, breeds freely in captivity and is justly celebrated for its beauty and personality.
Vriends

LENGTH: 39¼ inches (100 cm); this is the largest parrot in existence!

DISTRIBUTION: The interior of southern Brazil and western Bolivia, where the birds live in pairs or families along rivers. They feed primarily on palm nuts.

SPECIAL NOTES: Well-known in captivity, as it is an affectionate pet, although not a good talker. It dislikes strangers, however.

The first young was raised at the Bratislava Zoo in Czechoslovakia, in 1969. The chick died after two weeks.

Ralph Small of Brookfield, Illinois, is probably the only one who has had great success in the breeding and rearing of these majestic birds. His first pair was purchased from the Brookfield Zoo; he housed them in his basement in an enclosure of approximately 7' x 13'9" x 5'; as a nest box he used a 50-gallon steel drum half-filled with bark and a gallon of water to provide humidity. Mr. Small maintained a temperature of 77° to 79° F.

Genus: *Amazona* (Amazons)

These majestic birds live in an area that became famous for the mighty Amazon River, discovered by the Spanish explorer Francisco de Orellanda, in 1541. This river pours more than 59,000 gallons of water into the Atlantic Ocean in a single second! The Amazon River is far from clear, and its mud stains the ocean brown for more than 200 miles; this flow is caused by heavy tropical rains and melting snow in the Andes mountains. The Amazon River is almost 4,000 miles long and begins in the lakes of the Andes 18,000 feet above sea level, flowing eastward across the low plains of Brazil.

In this huge river-habitat 26 species (with their many subspecies) of Amazon Parrots live in the low, thick woodlands, open regions, swamps or coastal areas.

During the breeding season they live in pairs, but at other times large, noisy flocks can be observed. All birds have their own roosting place in the trees, and it is interesting to see the pairs stay together, even when they have no chicks to look after. Their breeding time occurs during our winter; they make their nests in a hollow limb or a hole in a tree.

The majority of the imported Amazons are young birds, sometimes half-tamed, but usually "right from the wild." It is no wonder, that they are nervous, noisy and suspicious. Leave them alone for a few days, offer them the proper food (along with what they are used to), and speak to them in a friendly way while feeding them. Older birds will not calm down as quickly as young Amazons. After their quarantine period however, they have usually settled down, and training can start.

Amazon Parrots are usually good talkers, although not all birds learn fast. I have known birds that learned to speak over 100 words, while others, after years of teaching, never managed more than two or three.

Amazons are the real "artists" among parrots, and are able to imitate; I have heard Amazon Parrots laugh, sneeze, whistle, imitate grandfather's

The Hyacinth Macaw *(Anodorhynchus hyacinthinus),* justly renowned for its great beauty, is friendly with those it knows, but tends to distrust strangers. In spite of its almost human, 'smiling' expression, the Hyacinth tends not to rate high in speaking capability. *Vriends*

smoker's cough or a squeaky door, or swear in many different languages! However, they never lose their somewhat harsh, natural voice, especially if we pay no attention to them.

Amazon Parrots are easy to keep, although this doesn't mean that you must buy a bird on impulse. Keep in mind that you are purchasing a friend for life!

I would love to see Amazon Parrots housed in large aviaries, where breeding successes may occur, but most aviculturists keep them in cages. Be sure you have a proper cage of at least 28 inches in length, constructed with strong metal bars, running horizontally. The shape must be rectangular as the birds become nervous in round cages!

Tame Amazons may be kept on a stand, with a wooden perch of 20 to 24 inches long with feeding cups on either side, and a 28-inch square platform underneath, with sand, for obvious reasons. Birds, kept on a stand, should be placed in a cage for the night.

If you have an aviary, supply the birds with a hollow tree trunk, barrels or boxes of hard timber, 24 x 24 x 24 inches, with an entrance of 6 inches in diameter. In front of the entrance attach some strong branches; on the inside fasten some mesh to the birds can leave the nest easily.

Although Chapter 3 of this book is devoted to feeding, we can say Amazon Parrots generally need the following: all sorts of sunflower seeds, oats, wheat, corn on the cob, some hemp and white seeds, millets (including spray millet), nuts, fruits, pear, bread, milk and willow, poplar, elder and fruit tree twigs. Imported birds must have cooked corn on the cob, boiled rice, germinated sunflower and canary seeds, and a rich variety of fruits (apples, pears, oranges, bananas, peaches, cherries, berries, etc.) The birds must gradually become accustomed to the foods recommended in Chapter 3.

It is against the law to keep the following species in captivity, as they are on the List of Endangered Species:
1. Bahama (Cuban) Amazon—*Amazona leucocephala bahamensis*
2. Puerto Rican Amazon—*Amazona vittata vittata*
3. St. Vincent Amazon—*Amazona guildingii*
4. St. Lucia Amazon—*Amazona versicolor*
5. Imperial Amazon—*Amazona imperialis*
6. Blue-cheeked Amazon—*Amazona dufresniana rhodocorytha*
7. Red-spectacled Amazon—*Amazona pretrei pretrei*
8. Vinaceous Amazon—*Amazona vinacea*
9. Red-necked Amazon—*Amazona arausiaca*
10. Yellow-shouldered Amazon—*Amazona barbadensis*
11. Red-tailed Amazon—*Amazona brasiliensis*

Orange-Winged Amazon *Amazona amazonica* (Linné)

DESCRIPTION: Predominantly green; the bird is similar to the Blue-fronted Amazon Parrot. The Orange-winged Amazon has blue lores, eyebrows and

Orange-Winged Amazon *(Amazona amazonica)* is a small species that is readily tamed and makes a pleasant pet.   *Vriends*

The Yellow-winged Blue-fronted Amazon *(Amazona aestiva xanthopteryx)* has probably been mistaken for the nominate form, the Blue-fronted Amazon for many years. It is likely that many are owned by persons completely unaware of their pets' true identity.   *Vriends*

Bodin's Amazon *(Amazona festiva bodini)*, is one of the rarer Amazon species. Only a few specimens can be found in captivity and breedings were also very infrequent.   *Vriends*

The Green-Cheeked Amazon *(Amazona viridigenalis)*, or Mexican Red Head, is yet another familiar member of this large genus. A pleasing personality is this bird's foremost asset for the bird fancier.   *Ebben*

218

forehead; the wing coverts are red, bend of the wing green, cheeks and crown as well as the wing primaries are yellow. Beak horn-colored with a dark tip. Iris orange, legs and feet gray.

LENGTH: 12¼ inches (31 cm)

DISTRIBUTION: Colombia, Venezuela, Guyana, Panama, Brazil, eastern Ecuador, northeastern Peru and Surinam. There are two subspecies.

SPECIAL NOTES: An extremely fine bird that becomes tame very quickly, when taken care of properly. Old birds tend to become moody, however.
This species is very popular in the United States, and according to T. Silva, a lutino specimen exists in northern California.

Blue-Fronted Amazon *Amazona aestiva* (Linné)

DESCRIPTION: Predominantly green, with a pale blue brow, the throat, cheeks and crown are yellow. Bend of wing yellow or red. The wing coverts are always red. The beak is gray. The iris orange, legs and feet gray.

LENGTH: 14½ inches (37 cm)

DISTRIBUTION: Brazil, Bolivia, Paraguay and northern Argentina. There are two subspecies.

SPECIAL NOTES: This Amazon Parrot is regularly available, and with reason, as the bird becomes very tame and affectionate. They are good talkers and mimics. Young birds are raised in nest boxes of 24 x 12 x 12 inches, or in old logs; diameter of entrance 6 inches. The female incubates the three to five white eggs for approximately 28 days. The chicks leave the nest box after 60 days.
At this moment there are pied yellow, blue and lutino mutations; the latter in the collection of my friend Dick Topper of California. Also the Musea Nacional of Sao Paulo has two lutinos from the same nest, from different years (probably from the same pair), found near a farm in do Baroneza de Mamaguape.

Bodin's Amazon *Amazona festiva bodini* (Finsch)

DESCRIPTION: Predominantly green; underparts with yellow shades. Brow and crown red, cheeks blue; lower back and rump red. Beak dark gray; iris orange. Legs and feet greenish-gray.

LENGTH: 13¼ inches (34 cm)

DISTRIBUTION: Venezuela and Guyana.

SPECIAL NOTES: There are only a few specimens in captivity; it was rarely bred. The only success, as far as I know, dates back to 1891: a Mr. Renouard of France had the good fortune to breed three young from a pair that a Mr. J. Abrahams of London had brought back from Buenos Aires.

Festive Amazon *Amazona festiva* (Linné)

DESCRIPTION: Predominantly green with red forehead and blue eyebrows and chin. Rump and back red. Beak light gray, iris orange, legs and feet greenish-gray.

LENGTH: 13¼ inches (34 cm)

DISTRIBUTION: Ecuador and Peru. There are two subspecies.

SPECIAL NOTES: Generally a good talker and mimic. It is, furthermore, interesting to note that yellow specimens exist. They could very well be lutinos (I have seen two specimens with red eyes and feet); however, it is a fact, that the natives of South America sometimes apply the secretion of a poisonous frog-species to the feathers, which then turn yellow. In this light it is also interesting to know the experience of Mr. Dieter Hoppe, who saw a yellow specimen that "could be this subspecies;" in any case this bird was believed to be treated with the above mentioned secretion from the frog's skin. The particular bird belongs to a Mr. Dutton. This method, called *tapiragem* in Brazil, is exclusively used on large parrots. It is known that, for example, the *A. finschi* and *A. viridigenalis* are often treated this way too, and even bleached on the head with a mild peroxide solution, which also turns the feathers yellow.

Green-Cheeked Amazon or Mexican Red-Head *Amazona viridigenalis* (Cassin)

DESCRIPTION: Predominantly green, with a red crown. The back feathers are edged with black. Blue eye-band. Blue tipped primaries and deep-red wing coverts. Bill horn-colored with a yellow shade; iris yellow, legs and feet gray-green. Immature birds have a red forehead.

LENGTH: 17 inches (43 cm)

DISTRIBUTION: Mexico.

SPECIAL NOTES: In 1934 this species (known for its intelligence and talking ability) hybridized with a Spectacled Amazon; three young were successfully raised. One chick was raised in South Africa (1976, Mr. B. Boswell of Natal); five in England (1979, Mr. J. Stoodley) and one in Holland (1980, Mr. W. Hoek); the latter aviculturist stated that the male is more heavily built than the hen, with much more red on the front. In 1981 Larry Brand (United States), according to Dr. Decoteau in a letter to my colleague Mr. H. H. Jacobsen (Denmark), raised five chicks.

Yellow-Cheeked Amazon *Amazona autumnalis* (Linné)

DESCRIPTION: Predominantly green, with blue-edged nape feathers. Lores and forehead are red. Crown blue. Usually some yellow beneath the eyes, and a reddish shade on the smaller primaries. Beak light gray with yellow on the

Red-Necked Amazon *(Amazona arausiaca).* The specimen shown here is a female. *Vriends*

The Lilacine Amazon *(Amazona autumnalis lilacina)* is a subspecies of the Red-lored Amazon *(A. autumnalis),* and a beautiful addition to any collection of birds. Its habitat is confined to western Ecuador and the Gulf of Guayaquil. *Vriends*

221

upper mandible. Iris orange; legs and feet greenish-gray.

LENGTH: 13¼ inches (34 cm)

DISTRIBUTION: Mexico, Honduras, Belize, Guatemala, Nicaragua, Colombia, Costa Rica, northwest Brazil and Ecuador. There are four subspecies.

SPECIAL NOTES: *Amazona autumnalis* is also known as the Primrose-cheeked Amazon, Scarlet-lored Amazon and Red-lored Amazon. These birds have a reputation of being poor talkers, but what they lack in imitative talents they make up for in appearance. They are undoubtedly one of the really majestic Amazon Parrots! "Red-lored Amazons," according to Dr. A. E. Decoteau, in his *Handbook of Amazon Parrots* (TFH-Publications, Inc., Neptune, N.J.), "have been bred and hatched in the United States. Hym Prenner has owned Amazons for years in central Iowa, and his favorite is the Red-lored Amazon. He claims he has never seen a mean Red-lored. To set up the birds for breeding, he took a small wine barrel which was well sealed, made a 14-inch hole in one side and equipped the barrel with a perch. He placed about one pound of peat in the bottom, then another two inches of wood shavings over the peat. He repeated this for each pair of Red-lored Amazons. His primary pair produced two eggs within a four-month period. Unfortunately, these eggs were infertile. It must be noted here that infertility in young first-time breeders is quite common. It seems to take Amazons a couple of nests before hatchability occurs. After three repeat tries, this pair of Red-lored Amazons successfully incubated and raised three babies. In total, Mr. Prenner hatched 22 baby Red-lored Amazons."

Little Double Yellow-headed Amazon
(Amazona barbadensis barbadensis)

222

Dufresne's Amazon or Granada Amazon *Amazona dufresniana* (Shaw)

DESCRIPTION: Predominantly green, with an orange-yellow forehead and lores. Blue tipped throat and cheek feathers. Orange speculum (the first four primaries); four inside tail feathers orange. Beak gray with some reddish shades at the base of the upper mandible. Iris orange-red; legs and feet gray. Immature birds lack the red forehead, have a green tail and orange wing coverts.

LENGTH: 13¼ inches (34 cm)

DISTRIBUTION: Guyana, Surinam and southeast Brazil. There are two subspecies.

SPECIAL NOTES: Purchased young, they become tame and talkative, but will never become famous as mimics. As far as I know there are no specimens in the United States.

Spectacled Amazon or White-Fronted Amazon *Amazona albifrons* (Sparrman)

DESCRIPTION: Predominantly green, with a white brow, red shades in the primaries, a blue crown and a scarlet eye region. All feathers are somewhat dark-edged. Beak yellowish, iris pale yellow, feet and legs light gray.

LENGTH: 10¼ inches (26 cm)

DISTRIBUTION: Mexico, Guatemala, Honduras, Costa Rica and Nicaragua. There are three subspecies.

SPECIAL NOTES: Very good talkers and mimics. In 1977, Mr. R. van Dieten of Holland raised one chick, two in 1978, three in 1979, and four in 1980. There is a lutino specimen in the Houston Zoo.

Cuban Amazon *Amazona leucocephala* (Linné)

DESCRIPTION: Predominantly green, with black-edged feathers; white brow, red throat and cheeks and a red patch on the belly. Beak horn-colored; iris green; legs and feet pink.

LENGTH: 12½ inches (32 cm)

DISTRIBUTION: Cuba, the Bahamas, the Cayman Islands, and the Isle of Pines. There are five subspecies.

SPECIAL NOTES: Once acclimatized this Amazon is hardy, gentle and a fair talker and mimic. Newly imported birds, however, are delicate. It is interesting to note that as early as summer 1885 the first hybrids were reported (*A. l. leucocephala* x *A. a. aestiva*) by a lady from Karlsruhe, Germany. Three chicks hatched from the four eggs, but only one young survived. The pair bred

Spectacled Amazons *(Amazona albifrons)*, or White-fronted Amazons, are smaller than most other Amazon species, but are very self-possessed and will stand up to the largest, most intimidating rival.   *Ebben*

A Tres Marias subspecies of the popular Double Yellow Head *(Amazona ocrocephala tresmariae).*   *Ebben*

224

again in 1886 and of the three eggs one was placed, thanks to the dentist, Dr. P. Hieronymous, under his breeding pair of Grand Eclectus; he had to assist however in freeing the chick from the egg (Prestwich in "Records of Parrots Bred in Captivity," pages 99-100, 1950-52). According to Mr. Dieter Hoppe all males have a narrow line of red feathers situated on the underside of the bend of the wing; this bend is green in females.

Yellow-Fronted Amazon *Amazona ochrocephala* (Gmelin)

DESCRIPTION: Predominantly green, with a yellow head with much variety in amount and intensity of color, often depending on the age of the bird; young birds have only a "yellow face." Underparts yellow shaded. Reddish or yellowish bend of wing. As you can see there is room for considerable color variation. Beak dark gray with yellowish-red on the sides of the upper mandible; iris orange-brown; legs and feet gray.

LENGTH: 13 inches (33 cm)

DISTRIBUTION: Colombia, Venezuela, Guyana, Surinam, Peru, Panama, Ecuador, Costa Rica, Mexico and Honduras. There are nine subspecies.

SPECIAL NOTES: Fine birds that become tame easily; they like to speak and imitate. They are regularly imported. For more details see the notes in GENUS.

Panama Amazon *Amazona ochrocephala panamensis* (Cabanis)

DESCRIPTION: Predominantly blue-green; almost identical to the nominate form, except for the yellow lower mandible and the yellowish brow. The black edges on the feathers are lacking.

LENGTH: 14 inches (36 cm)

DISTRIBUTION: Panama and Colombia.

SPECIAL NOTES: There is a blue mutant in the Wassenaar Zoo, The Hague, Holland; this specimen was paired to a green Panama, and they produced two split-colored chicks, in 1981. Two other blue birds were, according to T. Silva, imported to the USA from Colombia by Dr. Raymond Kray, but unfortunately one died. The remaining bird was then paired to a green Panama, resulting in two female offspring, currently seven years old (1982). Both youngsters are green (split) with a noticeable bluish cast to the underparts. Regretably, the blue specimen died before one of the offspring could have been paired to it.

Yellow-Shouldered Amazon *Amazona barbadensis* (Gmelin)

DESCRIPTION: Predominantly green; white face, yellow bordered. Yellow bend of wing, red wing coverts. Bill horn-colored, iris orange, feet and legs gray.

225

Imperial Amazon *(Amazona imperialis).* Vriends

The Cuban Amazon *(Amazona leucocephala palmarum),* a vigorously-protected member of the endangered species list. Vriends

LENGTH: 13 inches (33 cm)

DISTRIBUTION: Venezuela and Island of Aruba.

SPECIAL NOTES: This species is a rarity in captivity. Mr. Jose Santiago, from Puerto Rico, appears to have a singleton (1981). According to Ramon Noegel, the first 12 specimens were received in the United States in October, 1979, and all but two appeared to be males. According to information supplied by Mr. H. H. Jacobsen, the last specimen received by Mr. Noegel (January, 1981) was an old, decrepit female. She was placed with a male, purchased from the Gladys Porter Zoo. This pair nested in the latter part of June and early July; three eggs comprised the clutch; two proved to be fertile and were given to a foster parent for incubation. The pair began a second clutch with one egg being laid July 20th, and another on the 27th. The two eggs were hatched on the 26th and 27th of August, but the parents failed to raise the chicks. The old female has not started a new nest, and may be unable to do so, for when laparotomy was performed, she showed no sign of follicle development (laparotomy is a surgical incision through the flank). Two males are on loan from the San Diego Zoo and the Ellen Trout Zoo making a cooperative effort to captive-breed these rare Amazons.

St. Vincent's Amazon (Amazona guildingii) was named after Lansdown Guilding, a native of St. Vincent's and the Colonial Chaplain of that Island.

The Mealy Amazon *(Amazona farinosa)* is one of the largest of the Amazons. Despite his size and formidable appearance, he makes a personable pet and is very amenable to training.
Vriends

Hispanolan Amazon *(Amazona ventralis)*, a male of the species. *Vriends*

Mealy Amazon *Amazona farinosa* (Boddaert)

DESCRIPTION: Predominantly green; the feathers in the nape are black edged. On the back gray spots are shown; hence his name. Many adult birds have an orange-violet crown. Wing-coverts red. Beak yellowish horn-colored at the base, becoming dark towards the tip (Forshaw). The iris is reddish; legs and feet are pale gray.

LENGTH: 15 inches (38 cm)

DISTRIBUTION: Venezuela, Guyana, Surinam, Peru, Panama, Ecuador, Nicaragua, Costa Rica, Mexico, Guatemala and Honduras. There are five subspecies.

SPECIAL NOTES: Excellent talker and mimic. Dr. Decoteau raised two in 1979, and another two in 1981.

Hispaniolan Amazon *Amazona ventralis* (P.L.S. Müller)

DESCRIPTION: Predominantly green, with black-edged feathers. White brow and ring around the eye. Cheeks and crown blue, ear patches black. Reddish shade on the belly. Beak horn-colored, iris brown, legs and feet pink.

LENGTH: 11 inches (28 cm)

DISTRIBUTION: Santo Domingo

SPECIAL NOTES: According to W. de Grahl, these noisy birds are extremely delicate at first. Amusing and lively, they love all kinds of twigs, berries, and during the breeding and rearing period, mealworms as well. The species was first bred in 1971 (Jersey, England), and in 1979 at "Zoodom": the National Zoological Park of the Dominican Republic in Santo Domingo. They have reared young ever since; in 1981 six pairs were breeding in Royal-palm logs. R. Noegel gives a summary of the results of the breeding of this species at his Life Fellowship New Age Ranch in Florida; apparently the species has been bred for eight years into the second generation. A total of nineteen of these beautiful Amazons have been reared to maturity.

Lilac-Crowned Amazon or Finsch's Amazon *Amazona finschi* (Sclater)

DESCRIPTION: Predominantly green with a red brow and lores. Crown and nape blue; many feathers are black-edged. Beak horn-colored, iris orange, feet and legs greenish-gray.

LENGTH: 13 inches (33 cm)

DISTRIBUTION: Mexico. There are two subspecies.

SPECIAL NOTES: This is a regularly imported Amazon that was bred in the USA as early as 1949 by Mr. Mercer. Mr. R. E. McPeek of Ontario, Canada raised three young in 1972, three in 1973, and two in 1975. In that same year Mr.

Greenblatt of Poer Bird Farm in Arizona raised two chicks.

There are many "bleached" specimens in California, coming from Mexico, where they are known as "Lady Clairols."

Vinaceous Amazon *Amazona vinacea* (Kuhl)

DESCRIPTION: Predominantly green; the feathers of head, breast and back, but especially those of the nape, are black-edged. Red lores; wine-red on the breast; nape blue. Beak dull reddish; horn-colored towards the tip. Iris red; legs and feet pale gray. The female is much darker in color than the male; the beak is lighter.

LENGTH: 12 inches (30 cm)

DISTRIBUTION: Brazil and Paraguay.

SPECIAL NOTES: Nice, but reticent birds. They have been bred a few times in captivity (in 1977 by Mr. Clifford Smith, in 1978 by Mr. O. Poschung). In Britain a hybrid was bred by Messrs. J. and P. Stoodley (*A. a. salvini x A. vinacea*).

Genus: *Psittacus* (African Grey Parrots)

African Grey Parrot *Psittacus erithacus* (Linné)

DESCRIPTION: Predominantly gray with darker feather-edges and a red tail. Naked whitish face. Beak black, legs and feet dark gray. The female has the smaller head and beak, and her body is usually not as large as that of the male. The male has a round, yellow iris, the female's is elliptical.

LENGTH: 14¼ inches (36 cm)

DISTRIBUTION: Africa, especially in the forests of Angola, the Ivory Coast to and in the Congo, further in Fernanda Poa and Principe Island.

Well-known is the darker colored subspecies *P. e. timneh* (Timneh African Grey Parrot), from Guinea, Sierra Leone, Liberia and the western parts of the Ivory Coast (de Grahl).

SPECIAL NOTES: This widely-known species is an excellent talker and mimic. The care of this beautiful and affectionate parrot runs parallel with that of the Amazon Parrots.

House these fine birds in a roomy rectangular cage. For breeding you need a pair that is sexually mature, which means that the birds must be at least five to six years of age. Provide nest boxes of 16 x 18 x 26 inches. The entrance must be approximately 6 inches wide. The female incubates the two to three white eggs for 29 to 30 days. At first the male will feed his young while sitting in the nest entrance. He also visits his bride while she sits on the eggs to offer food. After approximately 10 weeks the young leave the nest, but will be fed by their parents for at least four months.

Lilac-Crowned Amazon *(Amazona finschi)* is also widely-known as Finsch's Amazon and is distinguished by the striking color and markings about the crown and lores. *Vriends*

The Vinaceous Amazon (*Amazona vinacea*), a typical Amazon species, is on the Endangered List and is strictly protected throughout its entire range. *Vriends*

231

The African Grey *(Psittachus erithacus)* is familiar to bird lovers the world over. His gray-scalloped body plumage and bright red tail are two of his physical hallmarks.
Ebben

232

Genus: *Poicephalus* (Senegal Parrots)

Yellow-Bellied Senegal Parrot *Poicephalus senegalus* (Linné)

DESCRIPTION: Predominantly green, with a dark gray head and bright yellor or orange-yellow breast and belly. The female is duller than the male, with yellow feathers throughout her complete "costume."

LENGTH: 9½ inches (24 cm)

DISTRIBUTION: West Africa, in three subspecies.

SPECIAL NOTES: Very popular birds, thanks to the fact that they quickly become tame and affectionate. They are even good talkers and mimics. They need the usual parrot foods and fruits during the breeding season, as well as nuts, oats and wheat. Due to their exceptionally strong bills it is advisable to purchase a strong rectangular cage, equipped with a thick, oak branch. Although the birds will breed in large cages, the best results will be obtained in an outdoor aviary with nest boxes of 12 x 12 x 20 inches (20 inches represents the height), with an entrance of 5 inches in diameter.

Another member of *Poicephalus* is the Meyer's Parrot (*P. meyeri*), from Africa, that is seldom offered for sale, but requires the same cage type and care.

The Senegal Parrot *(Poicephalus senegalus)* is the best-known member of his genus and has been familiar to aviculture for centuries. This bird, from central west Africa has three subspecies differing mainly in the color of the breast and lower abdomen.   *Vriends*

Blue-Headed Parrots *(Pionus menstruus)*, also known as Red-Vented Parrots, come from parts of Central and South America and are typical of the *Pionus species.* Somewhat smaller than the Amazons, these birds are noted for their very fine personalities and are a fine choice for a pet parrot. In this photo the male is at the right.   *Ebben*

Genus: *Pionus*

Blue-Headed Parrot or Red-Vented Parrot *Pionus menstruus* (Linné)

DESCRIPTION: Predominantly dark green, with a blue head and neck, and red under tail-coverts, tipped dark green. Black ear-coverts. Immature birds have a green-colored head and a light horn-colored beak. Adult birds have a dark gray beak with red near the base; the iris is brown; feet and legs are light gray.

LENGTH: 10½ inches (26.5 cm)

DISTRIBUTION: Trinidad, Costa Rica, Bolivia and Brazil.

SPECIAL NOTES: This very sociable bird is becoming very popular. As the majority of the imported birds are youngsters, much time must be devoted to acclimatization. I have, by the way, never come across good talkers!

Maximilian's Parrot (*P. maximiliani*) from eastern South America is spasmodically available and requires the same care.

Meyer's Parrot is a member of the genus *Poicephalus* and occurs in at least six subspecies. They are common in their African habitat and there have been recorded instances of captive breedings. The specimen shown here is *P. meyeri reichenow*. *Ebben*

To many experienced parrot lovers, the Yellow-Naped Amazon (*Amazona ochrocephala auropalliata*) is all that can be desired in a talking bird. His affinity for learning and pleasant personality have earned him fame in aviculture for over a century.

Vriends

Appendices

Periodicals

American Cage-Bird Magazine (monthly)
3449 North Western Avenue
Chicago, IL 60618 (USA)
Features a bi-monthly directory of Bird Societies

Avicultural Bulletin (monthly)
Avicultural Society of America, Inc.
734 North Highland Avenue
Hollywood, CA 90038 (USA)

Bird World (bi-monthly)
P.O. Box 70
No. Hollywood, CA 91601 (USA)

Cage and Aviary Birds (weekly)
Surrey House
1, Throwley Way
Sutton. Surrey, SM1 4QQ (England)
(Young birdkeepers under sixteen may like to join the *Junior Bird League*.
Full details can be obtained from the J. B. L., c/o *Cage and Aviary Birds*.

The A.F.A. Watchbird—American Federation of Aviculture Inc. (bi-
monthly)
P.O. Box 1125
Garden Grove, CA 92642 (USA)

Magazine of the Parrot Society (monthly)
24, Rowallan Drive
Bedford. (England)

Major Societies

Australia:
Avicultural Society of Australia
P.O. Box 48
Bentleigh East
Victoria

Canada:
Canadian Avicultural Society, Inc.
c/o Mr. E. Jones
32 Dromore Crescent
Willowdale 450
Ontario, M2R 2H5

Canadian Institute of Bird Breeders
c/o Mr. C. Snazel
4422 Chauvin Street
Pierrefonds, Quebec

Great Britain:
The Avicultural Society
c/o Mr. H. J. Horsewell
20 Bourbon Street
London W 1

New Zealand:
The New Zealand Federation of Cage Bird Societies
c/o Mr. M. D. Neale
31 Harker Street
Christchurch 2

United States of America:
Avicultural Society of America
(See *Avicultural Bulletin,* Pg. 237)

American Federation of Aviculture, Inc.
(See *The A.F.A. Watchbird,* Pg. 237)

Bibliography

Bates, Henry J. and Robert L. Busenbark. 1978. *Parrots and Related Birds.* TFH Publications, Inc. Neptune, New Jersey.

Bedford, Duke of. 1969. *Parrots and Parrot-Like Birds.* TFH Publications, Inc. Neptune, New Jersey.

Bosch, Klaus and Ursula Wedde. 1981. *Amazonen* (German - Amazons). Horst Müller Verlag. Walsrode. Bomlitz.

Forshaw, Joseph M. and William T. Cooper. 1978. *Parrots of the World.* David & Charles. Newton Abbot, London. 2nd (revised) edition.

idem: 1981. *Australian Parrots.* Landsdowne Press. Melbourne. 2nd edition.

Freud, Arthur. 1980. *All About the Parrots.* Howell Book House Inc. New York.

Greene, W. T. 1979. *Parrots in Captivity.* Updated by Dr. Matthew M. Vriends. TFH Publications, Inc. Neptune, New Jersey.

Harman, Ian. 1981. *Australian Parrots in Bush and Aviary.* Inkata Press. Melbourne and Sydney.

Kates, Steve. 1980. *Encyclopedia of Cockatoos.* TFH Publications, Inc. Neptune, New Jersey.

Low, Rosemary. 1972. *The Parrots of South America.* John Gifford Ltd. London.

idem: 1977. *Lories and Lorikeets.* Paul Elek. London.

idem: 1980. *Parrots - Their Care and Breeding.* Blandford Press Ltd. Poole. Dorset.

Pinter, Helmut. 1979. *Handbuch der Papageienkunde* (German - Handbook of Parrot Keeping). Franckh'sche Verlagshandlung. Stuttgart.

Rutgers, A. and K. A. Norris. 1972. *Encyclopedia of Aviculture,* Vol. 2. Blandford Press Ltd. Poole, Dorset.

Smith, George A. 1979. *Lovebirds and Related Parrots.* Paul Elek. London.

Vriends, Matthew M. 1978. *Encyclopedia of Lovebirds.* TFH Publications, Inc. Neptune, New Jersey.

idem: 1979. *Handboek voor de Liefhebbers van Australische Papegaaien en Parkieten* (Dutch - Handbook for Fanciers of Australian Parrots and Parakeets). Hollandia, Baarn.

idem: 1981. *Papegaaien en Parkieten uit Afrika, Azië en Zuid-Amerika* (Dutch - Parrots and Parakeets from Africa, Asia and South America). Kim/Hollandia. Baarn.

Books on Bird Diseases

Arnall, L. and J. F. Keymer, 1975. *Bird Diseases.* TFH Publications, Inc. Neptune, New Jersey.

Kronberger, Harry. *Haltung von Vögeln - Krankheiten der Vogel* (German - Bird Keeping - Bird Diseases). Gustav Fischer Verlag. Jena. 4th Edition.

Petrak, M. L. et al. 1969. Diseases of Cage and Aviary Birds. Bailliere Tindall (London) and Lea & Febiger (Philadelphia).